HOW TO MAKE MONEY TRADING

D0268372

To Cocoa, Cabana, Amber, Natasha and Rosie.
The best five dogs a man can have.

Published in the United Kingdom in 2012 by
Portico Books
10 Southcombe Street
London
W14 0RA

An imprint of Anova Books Company Ltd

ISBN 978-1-90844-914-6

A CIP catalogue for this book is available from the British Library.

10 9 8 7 6 5 4 3 2 1

Printed and bound by 1010 Printing International Ltd, China

This book can be ordered direct from the publisher at
www.anovabooks.com

Fully revised & updated

LEX VAN DAM

HOW TO MAKE MONEY TRADING

EVERYTHING YOU NEED TO KNOW TO CONTROL YOUR FINANCIAL FUTURE

PORTICO

CONTENTS

▶ Chapter 3

INTRODUCTION

You might have heard the old stock market saying, that when you give your money to an expert to manage, the expert ends up with your money and you end up being the expert. There is a lot of truth in that as far as I am concerned – giving my money to someone else to manage has seldom worked for me. That's why I manage my own money and that's why I think you should consider doing the same.

Over the past 19 years I have traded the stock market for myself as well as on behalf of a well-known international bank and a large hedge fund. My experiences have given me a deep understanding of what is really going on in the City of London. They formed the basis of a television series called *Million Dollar Traders*, which was shown on BBC2 in early 2009.

Million Dollar Traders followed a diverse group of eight people – five of whom were complete beginners and the other three were very inexperienced – trading stocks for a period of eight weeks, after only two weeks of training. Between them they traded with £500,000 (or $1,000,000 at the exchange rate at that time) of my own money, and were allowed to make their own decisions on what stocks to buy and sell.

Allowing eight people to manage my money with just two weeks' training seems a risky proposition, but I believed it to be safer than giving money to experienced professionals. This is because I believe that my methods of trading are based on common sense and can be easily learned and applied. And common sense is something that most experts lack!

The 'Million Dollar Traders' ended up losing about 2% of my capital, which does not sound great, but was much better than the professionals who, over the same period, lost more than 4%. I think it was pretty amazing that a group of inexperienced people with only minimal training were able to outperform the experts.

This book is not meant to teach you how to make a million dollars. It is intended to make you think about the markets, to explain a few basic and not-so-basic concepts, and to learn to trust yourself. After reading it you should have a good idea of what it takes to invest money in the stock market in a responsible manner.

More recently I have started my own trading academy at www.lexvandam.com, which helps people to trade, initially mainly through online modules. It is based on my concept of 5-Step-Trading® and has had a great reception from the people who have completed the modules.

Let me finish by repeating what my old manager at Goldman Sachs always used to say at the end of our morning meeting, 'Let's go make some money!'

Lex van Dam
www.lexvandam.com

TEN YEARS AGO I DON'T THINK THE
BANK WAS MATURE ENOUGH TO ACCEPT
PERFORMANCE-RELATED PAY.

BOB DIAMOND.
PRESIDENT OF BARCLAYS BANK

► Chapter 1

Know your market place

The financial world is complex and often misunderstood. Before you can start trading it is essential to know what and who you are dealing with.

The aim of this book is to provide a framework for making money out of trading stocks. Before the real fun starts in Chapter 2, you need to understand precisely how the financial system works, and where you fit in. If you want to be a player, first you have to know which game you are playing – good luck!

The world of finance

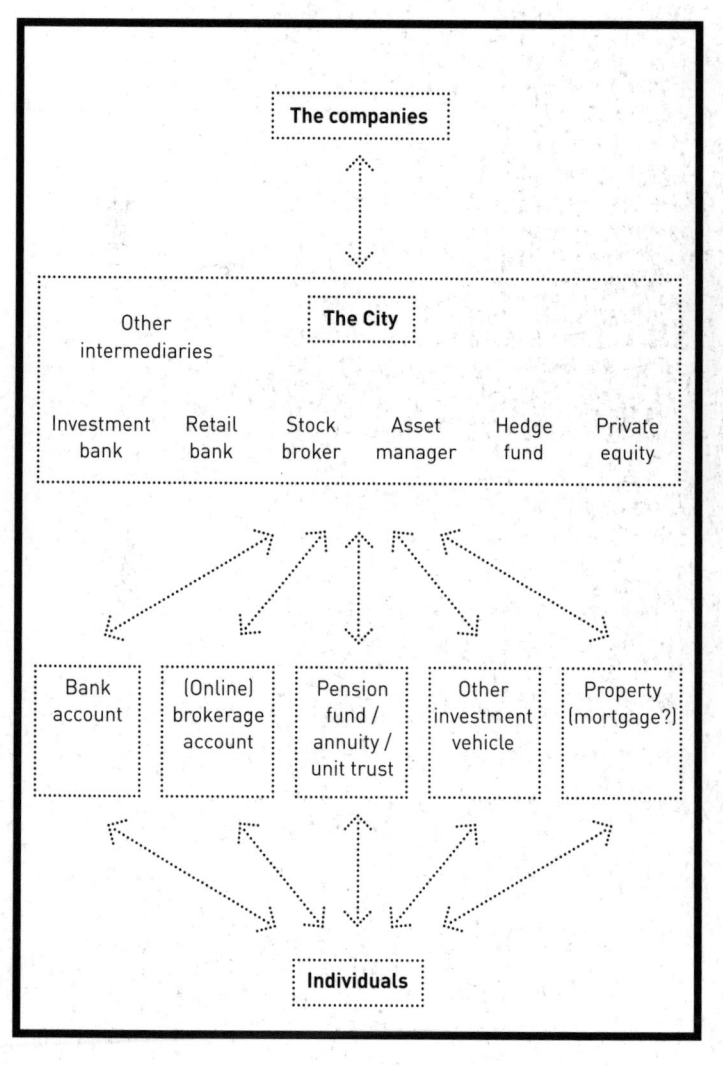

▶Companies

If you own a company and you want to develop a new product, build a new factory, or open new stores you might need to raise some money. If the numbers add up and your idea seems profitable, you will generally be able to raise this money either by borrowing it, or by selling a stake in your company.

That stake is called equity and, if the company is large enough, it can be traded on the stock market. Owning equity in a company gives the buyer the right to part of the profits, either directly through payment of dividends, or indirectly through retaining profits in the business and thereby making the company more valuable.

When you raise finance in the form of loans, this is called debt or a bond. The money that a company makes is first used to pay interest on these loans, and any residual money belongs to the shareholders, and can be used to pay them a quarterly or annual dividend.

Bond

Issued by a government or a company to raise money. Interest ('coupon') is repaid every year (or quarter) until maturity when the principal is repaid. If you own a bond you are lending money to the company; you are not an owner as you would have been if you had bought some equity. This means you take less risk but you don't have the same upside as if you owned the equity.

Equity

A stake or share in the ownership of a company.

COMMON MISCONCEPTION: Following a set of trading rules will make you money

There are plenty of so-called investment 'gurus' out there who will try to convince you that all you need to make money is to follow their rules. I believe strongly that you cannot simply learn a set of trading rules and expect to make money. If you are lucky this may work for a while, but there will come a point when the trading environment changes and the old rules stop working, and without a new set of rules you are stumped. You need to develop a trading style that suits you, with your own rules that must be flexible.

This book does not contain a list of rules to be followed blindly, instead it offers general guidelines that can be adapted depending on your own circumstances and knowledge, as well as the prevailing market environment.

When making trading decisions many people simply look at historical stock movements and try to use these to predict future stock prices. Others just analyse individual companies rather than the wider context in which they trade. I take a holistic approach to trading and try to cover all the different bases before making my decisions ... I think you should too.

MY AIM IS TO MAKE YOU THINK AND CHALLENGE CONVENTIONAL WISDOM AND THIS BOOK PRESENTS A FRAMEWORK THAT YOU CAN USE TO MAKE BETTER INVESTMENT DECISIONS.

Buying a share gives you a right to part of all the future revenue streams of a company, and it is interesting to know that equity investors look at the same company in a different way to bond investors. Bond investors want to ensure their interest is paid on time and that their initial capital is paid back when the loan terminates. They are very focused on analysing the cash flows of a company. Equity investors are more about hope; they hope that the company will make money and that the share price will go up. Their investment is a lot riskier than simply lending money to the company but the potential rewards are a lot higher as well. Companies are not the only ones to issue bonds. The UK government raises funds by issuing bonds known as Gilts. So even if you feel far removed from the world of finance you, as a taxpayer, are a player whether you like it or not.

This book focuses on shares, rather than bonds, currencies, or commodities, although you will see later that the stock market also allows you to trade these assets in exactly the same way as you would trade an ordinary share.

▶ The City

When the UK's stock market was a physical market place, it was based in the City of London. The term 'The City' is now a shorthand name for Britain's financial centre. After New York, the City is the world's second largest financial centre.

People inside the City like to think that its role is crucial to the operation of the world economy. Unfortunately, this overwhelming sense of self-importance has lead to the City, and other financial centres around the world, developing from 'innocent' service providers into monsters that can potentially bring down the world financial system. My view is that the City has still not realised that it can only survive long term, if the government (ultimately the voters) still believes it is in the best interest of the country, and because both people and companies decide to continue to use the services it provides. In the meantime, whatever your view of the City, you need to come to terms with the facts of life in the financial world, and deal with them in a productive manner. You need to understand the way it functions and how it makes money before you can make money yourself. There are a number of different players in the City. How they form a link between companies and individuals is illustrated in the diagram on p.9.

▼ Retail banks

The retail banks that are found on the high street have millions of customers. These comprise individuals, with a wide range of income and wealth, as well as businesses.

If you have your money on deposit or in a savings account at your local high street bank, or via Internet banking, the chances are that this money is not sitting in a safe waiting for you to ask for it back. It gets moved to the head office of the bank, which is part of the City, and is used to lend to other people and companies, or is invested in government bonds or in one of a huge variety of investment vehicles. Retail banks make their money from the difference between the rates of interest they pay for money that is deposited with them, and the rates they charge when they lend money to individuals and companies. They also make fees when they sell investment products to their clients. Retail banks tend to lend out money for the longer term and borrow it short term. Deposits are really nothing else than short-term loans from you to the bank. If deposit holders no longer trust their bank and want to withdraw their money, this causes huge problems, as the money simply isn't available. It has been lent out for the longer term in the form of company loans or mortgages that are not easily converted back into cash in the short term. This shortage of cash can cause a panic or a run on the bank, and usually the government will intervene and take control of the bank in order to stabilise the situation – you might remember the queues outside the branches of Northern Rock in September 2007. Many Northern Rock shareholders held onto their stock until it was worthless. Had they understood the business of Northern Rock they might well have avoided this.

Names to know: Barclays Bank

Barclays Bank (1690–) was founded by John Freame and Thomas Gould under the name of Goldsmith bankers in Lombard Street in the City of London. The black spread eagle corporate logo dates back as far as 1728.

In 1736 James Barclay, John Freame's son-in-law, became a partner in the business. His family name became the official name of the bank in 1896, when a merger took place with 19 other banks, to form Barclay and Company Limited. Between them the group had 182 branches and deposits of £26 million. These banks were connected by a web of family and religious links, and the bank was often referred to as the Quaker Bank.

The bank expanded rapidly throughout the UK and abroad, especially in Africa, the Middle East and the West Indies. In 1961 Barclays opened Britain's first computer centre for banking in Drummond Street, London and in 1966 it launched the UK's first credit card, Barclaycard. Barclays re-introduced the Automated Teller Machine (ATM) with great success at its Enfield branch in 1967. The first ATM had been developed in 1939 in New York, but was closed down after six months, because customers did not trust it and thus did not use it.

In 2000 Barclays took over mortgage-provider the Woolwich, and in early 2007 the bank tried to become a global banking powerhouse by taking over Dutch bank ABN Amro. The fact that this take-over failed was probably lucky for Barclays as the global financial crisis was about to set in. In 2008 Barclays bought the core business of US bank Lehman Brothers, which was then merged with Barclays own investment banking business, Barclays Capital. Barclays had a stock market valuation of about £10 billion at the end of Feb 2009, more than an 80% decline of its peak value in 2007. However by January 2012 this had recovered to about £25 billiion. The firm employs just under 150,000 people.

▼ Investment banks

Investment banks differ from retail banks because they don't have branches on the high street. Their clients tend to be large companies or extremely wealthy individuals. Goldman Sachs and Morgan Stanley are two of the most famous investment banks in the world. Some banks have both a retail arm and an investment banking arm, such as Barclays and HSBC.

Investment banks comprise many departments that all aim to make a profit for the bank. There is virtually no part of the investment process that investment banks do not control or participate in. Here we will examine just the equity-related areas of an investment bank, and ignore foreign exchange, commodities, such as oil and copper, and fixed income instruments such as bonds.

▷ Agency business

This part of the bank deals with stocks and shares. The equities division of an investment bank generally consists of research analysts, traders and salespeople. This part of the bank aims to generate commission through execution of client orders.

The research analysts tend to be sector specialists and publish research on large companies. The client, often a pension fund or another large institution, will speak to the research analyst to get an idea of the fundamental views on the companies that the analyst follows. The salesperson will try to convert this analysis and advice into actual orders so that the bank can charge commission when the trader executes the order on the exchange. The trader might take an additional fee as well to be compensated if he takes risk himself.

▷ Proprietary business

Some investment banks have an area where they take positions in shares for their own account. This is called principal investing or proprietary trading. Sometimes it takes the shape of private equity, which is discussed below. There are certain risks involved but these ventures tend to generate a great deal of money for the bank. If they do very badly the department will be closed down, but will usually start up again a few years later, because memories are short in investment banking and it can be so profitable for those involved.

▷ Corporate finance

The corporate finance area helps companies raise money for ventures such as take-overs. Corporate finance can use the agency business salespeople to try to sell shares of a company to large institutions. If they are able to place an issue of shares successfully, the bank will be paid a commission, which is usually between 2% and 5%. Corporate finance also gives strategic advice to companies on how to run their business in a way that the stock market will like and helps them with mergers and acquisitions. All these activities make vast sums of money for the bank.

There are many potential conflicts of interest here. That is why investment banks are obliged to maintain 'ethical walls' to prevent the agency and proprietary businesses gaining access to the price-sensitive information that corporate finance obtains.

▶ ▶ The inside track   **Investment banks**

As you can see, investment banks take very little risk. Only in the proprietary businesses do they really trade on their own account. The rest are all fee-paying businesses. When you deal with them either as an individual or as a company, you are the one who takes the risk and you are the one who ends up paying the fees, either directly or indirectly. This is important, because if you think that bankers are paid because they take risks you are wrong, they get paid because they are the system – just like the owners of a casino. If you want to invest or trade to build a pension, you must realise you are not the house, you are just a visitor. If you are not careful your hard-earned money will just be the oil that keeps the machine running.

▷ Other activities
Investment banks may also own asset management companies as described in the section below or structure investment products that are aimed at large investors such as life insurance companies, company pension schemes, or for large groups of retail investors. They can use research that is produced within their own investment bank but are often a client of other banks as well.

▼ Asset management companies
Asset management companies do just that – they manage money for their clients and charge a fee for this service. They tend to offer different investment options. There is a wide variety of funds with different styles and different portfolio managers. Some funds are themed and may specialise in a particular country, such as China, others may be benchmarked against the UK market, and aim to outperform the FTSE 100 for example.

Asset managers are usually large companies with a lot of buying power, which means they pay their service providers low commissions, and have access to the best research available. Clients tend to choose their asset manager on the basis of the historical performance of the investment funds that the firm manages. The upshot is that all these funds copy one another because no one wants to go out on a limb, even if they turn out to be wrong in the end.

▼ Hedge funds
Hedge funds have been in the news a great deal recently and their reputation has taken a battering. At a basic level, hedge funds are asset management companies that use a variety of different strategies to make money, including the strategy of short selling (see pp.33–35).

There are many different types of hedge funds. Some funds use computer models to make their buying decisions and have no interest in what the companies they invest in actually do, some analyse the companies they invest in to the nth degree, while others invest in art or property rather than stocks. However, all of

Life is not always fair if you are trying to do the best thing for your investors. Take for example Tony Dye, a famous fund manager from Philips & Drew Funds Management (PDFM), a large UK asset management company. Tony Dye was concerned that the market was starting to become overvalued and he wanted to protect his clients against a potential crash. Unfortunately his timing was off and clients started to complain to PDFM that managers at other companies were making more money. The clients started to leave, and PDFM management fired 'Dr Doom', as Tony was known by then. Shortly after that, the market did take a dive, and Tony was proven right. PDFM management looked foolish and so did the clients. Those who moved their money to higher performing funds got hit hardest when the market crashed. When you read disclaimers that state 'past performance does not predict future performance' you had better believe it!

them have a similar compensation structure. They make money for themselves by charging a management fee and a performance fee. Hedge funds have grown dramatically over the last ten years and they are not all run by talented people. However, as long as investors stick around, a less able manager is not going to volunteer that information!

▼ Private equity

Private equity is a wide term. At its simplest level it means owning equity in companies not listed on the stock exchange. There has been a great deal of activity in this area over the past decade.

The way I think it works (although I am sure a private equity professional would disagree), is that private equity borrows cheap money from the banks, and then buys up companies. The companies are then restructured, after which those involved in the venture often pay themselves a huge dividend. This type of activity is all well and good when the economy does well and cheap money is available, but when the tide turns these companies often have a large debt load and fail to keep up with the interest payments on this debt, and the employees lose their jobs. Private equity tends to take away the 'fat' in a company in pursuit of profit.

Names to know: Alfred Winslow Jones

Alfred Winslow Jones (1901–1989) founded the world's first hedge fund in 1949. It still exists today as a fund of fund, i.e. a vehicle that invests in other hedge funds as opposed to managing the assets itself. A. W. Jones published an article in *Fortune* in 1949 called 'Fashions in Forecasting'. While writing this article he realised that market direction is very hard to predict, either up or down, and that an investor should instead be focusing on building a hedged portfolio with a focus on picking stocks.

As he was more of an intellectual than an investor, Jones soon realised he needed help. To attract top-quality investment management, he introduced the concept of paying a 20% performance fee to his managers, which is still the standard today. Instead of focusing on picking stocks, he started picking investment managers, allocating capital amongst them according to performance and risk parameters. The managers only got paid when they made money. His investors apparently lost money in only three out of 34 years that he managed his fund.

He also believed that people who understand the intricacies of short selling make better long-only managers than those who do not. In an interview in 1966 he responded to investors who regarded short selling with suspicion by saying that he was using 'speculative techniques for conservative ends'. Forty years later the same suspicions still exist.

I heard a story about a big European investment bank whose private equity arm had always been regarded as a *wünderkind*. When they met with the Board, the question was not whether they had made money in the last quarter, but how much. At a meeting in early 2009 the guy in charge of the division was asked what the balance sheet of one of his largest investments looked like – he was not able to answer. He was then asked if he thought he should know these things. Clearly he was utterly embarrassed, lost all the confidence of his management, and subsequently his job. How can you be responsible for investing hundreds of millions (or billions) of pounds in companies and then not know what shape your investments are in? Unfortunately the people who did best in the good times were those who took the most risk and no one questioned them. The bottom line is that in the good times nobody asks the right questions and in bad times you are not going to get the right answers. Be very careful when you invest in hedge funds or private equity.

▼ Brokers

Brokers can form part of the agency business in an investment bank where they are known as salespeople (or salestraders), or they can exist as a separate firm. Brokers execute trades on the stock exchange, either electronically, or by finding a party that is

Broker

A party who acts as an agent in the buying or selling of a stock. These agents need to be registered with the appropriate government bodies. There are three potential levels of services.

Execution-only service

Where the client makes all decisions, broker just executes.

Advisory service

Where the client decides, broker gives advice on specific shares.

Discretionary service

Where the broker makes decisions on behalf of the client.

interested in taking the other side of a trade. Some arrange deals between large parties only; others will take clients of any size. Some give advice and provide research but their main aim is for you to pay them commission.

Online brokers tend only to execute orders on your behalf. Traditional brokers may want to give you advice about what shares to buy and sell, or may simply execute your orders on your behalf.

▶ ▶ The inside track **Brokers**

My advice is to listen and learn but not to follow individual stock advice and never to give discretion to your broker. Often these brokers are only allowed to recommend shares based on research that their firm has approved. This is to avoid the client suing the firm if things go wrong. However, your broker will probably give most of their clients exactly the same advice as they give you. This means that by the time you have received their advice the stock might already have been bought by several other people and risen in value. My view is you need to do your own research and decide for yourself.

Sometimes brokers ask for total discretion, which means trading in your account and on your behalf, without having to ask your permission for every trade they execute. Not everybody can be a broker; brokers need to be registered with the Financial Services Authority, and have a certain amount of regulatory capital in their business. People who speak directly to clients are required to pass exams to show they are competent. If you have a criminal record it is unlikely that you will be accepted as a broker. A broker is paid according to the volume of transactions he or she undertakes.

▶ Individuals

It should be clear by now that the City does have an impact on your life, whether you like it or not. Let's have a look at where and when you become involved with the City:

1. Bank accounts
Retail banks provide current and savings accounts, mortgages, investment products and share dealing services. As well as earning money in the way described earlier in this chapter, retail banks demand charges for all their services, and they also apply penalty charges in certain instances, for instance when your account becomes accidentally overdrawn.

2. Share dealing accounts
If you already have a share dealing account, either online or with a broker, every instruction you give to buy or sell a share, ends up somewhere in the City. Brokers act as the agent between you and the stock market. They have technical expertise and are able to hold your money so that you can pay for your shares.

3. Unit trusts and life insurance
If you have money in a unit trust, or a life insurance policy or annuity, or a so-called guaranteed product, this will have been sold to you and/or is managed by someone who represents a City institution. These institutions offer an enormous array of products

and will market the best performers to their customers in the hope of attracting a large volume of business. They will sell you the Brazil story or the alternative energy story or whatever they think will generate commissions. This is obviously not necessarily what is best for you or what will do best in the future.

Some of the managers are active and buy and sell stocks regularly. They tend to have their own research departments. Other managers are passive and believe that they cannot outperform, say the FTSE 100, and spend hardly any time on research. Both will charge fees (yes, there are always fees), but the latter are much lower as their organisations are smaller, and therefore their costs are also lower.

4. Pension funds
These are the key to your future. Pension funds can be managed internally by the companies that employ you, but more often than not, they are managed by an asset manager in the City. Unfortunately there are increasing numbers of instances where pension plans have been improperly funded, with shortfalls left, right and centre, even though these are often hidden behind actuarial assumptions. There is a lot of research on pensions these days as the state of the pension plan makes a huge difference to the valuation of a company. Building your own pension now seems a better option than ever, and being able to understand how to invest might help you tackle this important issue.

5. Hedge funds and private equity
If you have invested in one of these this will once again connect you to the City. Even if you are not knowingly invested your pension fund might be, or even a charity that you contribute to.

WHEN YOU UNDERSTAND HOW THE CITY WORKS YOU WILL BE ABLE TO PROTECT YOURSELF.

Names to know: Sir John Templeton

Sir John Templeton (1912–2008) was an American fund manager who is widely recognised as one of the most successful investors of the 20th century. He started his career at a brokerage company in New York, before launching his own investment management firm, which was a pioneer of the unit trust (mutual fund in the US) industry.

He is best known for his main fund, Templeton Growth. Under his management it was the top-performing fund amongst its competitors averaging returns of more than 15% over 45 years; if you had invested $100,000 with him in 1954 and had not taken any money out, it would have been worth over $60 million by the year 2000. He has been described as 'arguably the greatest stock picker of the century'.

Sir John Templeton was very much a fundamental investor and started investing overseas many years before most of his US contemporaries. A notable example of his success is his early investment in Japan, before the market there entered a long-term bull market, and his exit before it collapsed.

A deeply religious member of the Presbyterian Church he became very well known for his philanthropic activities. The John Templeton Foundation, established in 1987, has as its mission statement to: 'serve as a philanthropic catalyst for discovery in areas engaging life's biggest questions. These questions range from explorations into the laws of nature and the universe to questions on the nature of love, gratitude, forgiveness and creativity'. The Foundation has roughly $1.5 billion in assets. In 2007 it handed out grants to a value of approximately $70 million.

►The stock market

In the UK stocks trade on the London Stock Exchange (LSE) where all the buy and sell interests come together. For instance, one pension fund may decide to sell a stock because they feel the price will fall in the short term, while another fund will regard this as a good buying opportunity, as they believe the stock to be good value in the long term. Historically, transactions took place in a physical market place where people shouted out bids and offers, but these days most stock exchanges operate electronically.

Top global stock markets (listed companies only)	
Country	Value (US$, December 2011)
United States	15.1 trillion
Japan	3.5 trillion
China	3.4 trillion
United Kingdom	3.1 trillion
Hong Kong	2.1 trillion
Canada	1.9 trillion
France	1.5 trillion
Germany	1.3 trillion
Australia	1.3 trillion
Brazil	1.3 trillion

The value of Canadian and Australian markets is higher than you might expect because many of their companies produce raw materials, a sector that has done very well over the past ten years. Many companies in Germany are in private hands so the overall value might be lower than expected.

Stock exchange

A market place for shares where buyers and sellers come together.

▼Stock market deregulation

The LSE used to have a near monopoly for UK shares, but from the end of 2007 a European Directive (Market in Financial Instruments Directive (MiFID)) put an end to this. You can now trade UK shares on many alternative electronic exchanges, with unusual names such as POSIT, Chi-X and Turquoise, often at lower prices than previously possible. On a practical basis, this makes no difference to the retail investor, as it is the stockbroker who is responsible by law for best execution ensuring that you do get the best price. You can imagine what a headache it is for these brokers to do this. The competition between all the new exchanges was one of the factors in sending down shares in the LSE as seen below.

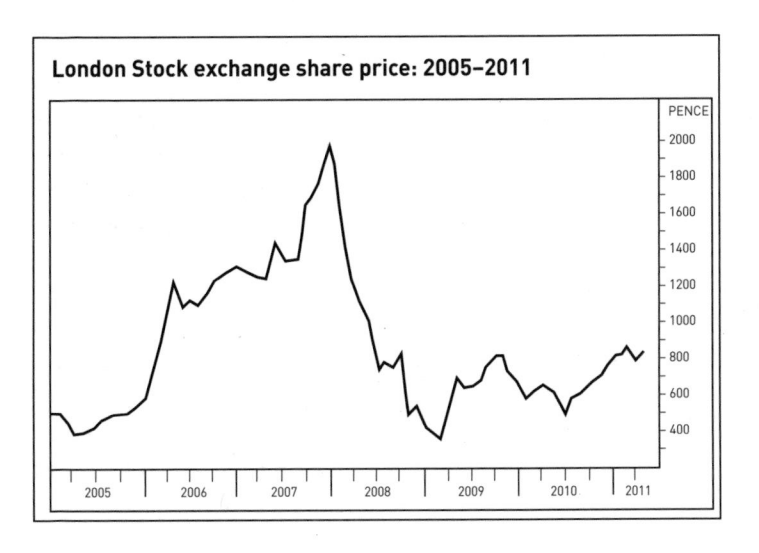

London Stock exchange share price: 2005–2011

▼ Financial regulation

Obviously a system like this where so much money is at stake needs a referee who ensures that the rules of play are developed and enforced. The body that regulates the financial services industry in the UK is called the Financial Services Authority (FSA). One of its aims is to promote efficient, orderly and fair markets to ensure that the public maintains confidence in the financial system – something that is easier said than done.

▶ Trading on the stock market

Before you are ready to invest and trade in shares you need to be aware of the products available and the strategies you can use to trade on the stock market.

▼ Stocks and shares

Let's first look at 'ordinary' shares in more detail. If you buy one share of a company at £2.30 you will have one vote at the Annual General Meeting. That may feel quite empowering. However, one share does not amount to much if there are 9 billion shares altogether, meaning that there are 9 billion votes held by hundreds of thousands of shareholders. Most people never bother to vote. They hold the stock in the hope it will go up over time and to cash in the dividend that it pays each quarter. Let's say the dividend it pays per stock is about 4.6p (2% of £2.30). This is known as a 2% dividend yield per year. Giving an order to your broker to buy an ordinary share is the old fashioned way of purchasing a stock. Buying a stock is also known as 'going long' or initiating a long position.

▼ Buying stocks

When opening your brokerage account you will be asked a number of questions regarding your personal experience and the amount of money you can invest. They are keen for you not to lose all your money on day one as their commission flow will end then and there. When you contact your broker with an order, either via the

---

Annual general meeting (AGM)

An AGM is generally held every year to inform shareholders about how the company is doing. The company's accounts are presented and resolutions are passed. Questions can be asked by all shareholders, no matter how small.

Internet, by phone or in person, the first thing he or she will do is check to see if there is enough money in your account.

If you have the necessary funds, the order will be executed on the (electronic) stock exchange, and the broker will ensure the share is held in your name. The proof of ownership also tends to be electronic these days. For this service you pay the broker a fee called commission. This can be as high as 1% when you are given personal advice or as low as five basis points (100 basis points is 1%) on the Internet. Broking is a volume business: the more you trade the more money they make.

Before you buy a share you also need to find out the exact code for the stock. For example, Microsoft trades under symbol MSFT, Barclays under BARC LN or BARC.L. Your broker will be able to help you with this or you can do a search on the Internet.

Transaction cost

A commission payable to the broker to pay for their services.

Most people are aware of having to pay a £30 overdraft penalty on their current account as it is clearly shown on a bank statement. However, when you have a share dealing account these charges are much less transparent and can add up really quickly; make sure you check the small print.

▼ Share indexes

The larger stocks on a stock exchange often form part of an index. This index contains a certain number of stocks, and the level of the index is usually calculated by giving large stocks a bigger weighting than smaller stocks. If the index goes up 1%, it means that the average stock in the index went up by 1%, and not that all stocks rose by 1%. The index gives you a quick market snapshot of the performance of the average stock.

USA	S&P 500
USA	Dow Jones Index
USA	Nasdaq 100
UK	FTSE 100
France	CAC40
Germany	DAX30
Japan	Nikkei 225
Hong Kong	Hang Seng Index
Europe	DJ Euro Stoxx 50 Index

As well as indexes that follow the performance of the largest stocks, such as the FTSE 100 in the UK, there are also sector indexes that will tell you how stocks have fared within a particular sector.

The Stoxx 600 is a broad index of 600 large stocks in Europe, including the UK, and has sub-indexes that are sector based and include:

Insurance (for example Prudential)
Basic Resources (Rio Tinto)
Banks (HSBC)
Construction (CRH)
Chemicals (BASF)
Travel & Leisure (Ryanair)
Oil & Gas (BP)
Financial Services (Deutsche Boerse)
Telecoms (France Telecom)
Industrials (BAE Systems)
Technology (Nokia)
Media (Reed Elsevier)
Autos (BMW)
Retail (Hennes & Mauritz)

Food & Beverages (Unilever)
Personal & Household Goods (BATS, Philips)
Utilities (National Grid)
Health Care (GlaxoSmithKline)

When doing your research, these indexes can give a good overview of how a sector has performed relative to the market, or a company to its sector. Over time, as companies grow or decrease in value, the composition of these indexes changes. Any such rebalances tend to take place at regular times throughout the year, for example quarterly.

In December 2011 the value of all the companies that trade on stock markets worldwide was about $46 trillion. This is about 30% less than it was at the end of 2007. To give you an idea of its relative size, the value of all the products and services that the world produces each year (world GDP) is about $63 trillion. As mentioned above, UK listed companies are worth about $3.1 trillion. The US is about five times as big at $15.1 trillion.

NEARLY A THIRD OF THE VALUE OF THE WORLD'S LISTED COMPANIES IS BASED IN THE UNITED STATES.

Index

A single number that represents the performance of an underlying number of securities. The FTSE 100 shows the performance of the largest 100 UK listed companies. In France they use the CAC 40, in Germany the DAX 30, Japan has the Nikkei 225, and in the US the best known indexes are the Dow Jones, the S&P 500 and the technology based Nasdaq 100.

Market capitalisation

The total market value of a public company. It equals the stock price multiplied by the number of shares outstanding. FTSE 100 stocks are qualified as large cap stocks as opposed to mid-cap and small cap stocks.

The Top 10 FTSE 100 and S&P 500 companies (Dec 2011)

FTSE 100	£ Billion Market Cap
Royal Dutch	146
BHP Billiton	121
HSBC	92
BP	89
Vodafone	87
GlaxoSmithKline	72
Rio Tinto	69
Unilever	65
British American Tobacco	58
BG Group	47

S&P 500	$ Billion Market Cap
Exxon Mobil	387
Apple	363
IBM	227
Microsoft	215
Chevron	208
Wal-Mart	203
Google	202
Berkshire Hathaway	194
General Electric	177
Johnson & Johnson	173

To put the current situation in perspective, Exxon Mobil was worth $490 billion in 2007 and has lost about 20% of its value since then. General Electric was worth about $440 billion in 2007 and has only just stayed in the top 10 after losing about 60% of its value.

▼ Trading versus investing

In theory, investing is buying stocks with the intention of holding them over the long term, while trading generally has a shorter time frame. In my world investing and trading are the same. I would not hold on to a stock long term if it starts to lose money, as I would assume that either my analysis, or my timing is wrong. Getting rid of bad positions should be regarded as a positive rather than a negative thing – it is never advisable to hold onto a stock at a massive loss in the hope that it will start to go up again in the long term. However, you do need to know what time horizon suits your trading style, and that is discussed in a later chapter.

▼ Contracts for difference (CFDs)/ spread betting

When you invest you normally buy shares but if you want to make money you do need to have the ability to 'short'. Short selling is selling a share that you don't own in the hope of buying it back at a later date at a lower price (see below). That is where CFDs or spread betting comes in.

CFDs allow you to take a bet on a share price going down. They can be useful as well if you want to go long (i.e. buy a share) because you need less cash to get the same exposure and you don't pay the stamp duty, which is currently 0.5% (always check as this can be subject to change). Spread betting also means that your profits are not subject to capital gains tax.

Caution. Be very careful when you spread bet as you do not need to put up all the cash yourself, and this can lead to excessive risk taking. That is fine when everything is going well, but it is very addictive, and if you have a very large leveraged position when things take a turn for the worst, you could get totally wiped out. If you own a stock and have paid for it in full and the stock were to halve, you would still have 50% left; if you had leveraged twice you would be left penniless. Also make sure you check the charges that you pay when borrowing the money – the chances are that they are higher than the returns you will end up making.

▼ Short selling

Short selling is currently a hot topic and has often been blamed for sharp falls in company share prices. The perception is that (groups of) speculators sell the shares short, then spread false rumours about the company to create a panic, which then causes the stock price to go down, and the short sellers then buy back the stock and make a profit. This is called a bear raid.

Short selling rules were introduced in the UK banking sector in September 2008 to stop the dramatic falls in share prices. Unfortunately this did not have the desired effect as it only temporarily addressed some of the symptoms of a failing and incompetent bank management and the banking sector lost more

Short selling

Selling a stock that the seller does not own at the time of the sale (i.e. the stock is borrowed). The goal is later to buy that stock back at a lower price, thus making a profit on the trade, before giving the stock back to the party it was borrowed from. Short selling can be for outright profit motives or to hedge a position and thus reduce risk.

than half its value over the next five months anyway. Short selling is used for two reasons:

1. 'Naked' short selling
When short selling is used to reflect the trading view that an individual stock is going down in value.

2. Hedging
Let's say you don't think a stock is necessarily going down, you just think that this stock is not as cheap as another stock in the same sector. For example you might think BP is a better bet than Shell. In that case you can take a long position in BP and a short position in Shell. The thinking is that you don't mind if both stocks go up, you just want BP to do better than Shell, and you think that just going long BP is too risky in case the market goes down, and you want to protect yourself, i.e. 'hedge' your bet by selling Shell short.

▶ ▶ The inside track   **Short selling**

I believe the ability to short sell is an integral part of any investment strategy as long-only portfolios and pensions are completely at the mercy of stock market fluctuations. Short selling offers flexibility in times of stock market turbulence and it is time that it is properly understood and generally accepted.

Some people say that it is wrong to sell a company's shares short as you will cause economic misery for others. The fact is that if a company's management were incompetent, or if the industry were in terminal decline, its share price would fall anyway. And, if your analysis is wrong, the stock price will not go down, and your short selling strategy will backfire. Spreading false rumours is obviously illegal, but there are instances when investors will analyse a company and conclude that the stock price is far above its fundamental value. Let's view this from the other side. If, after careful analysis, you decided that a stock was too cheap, you would buy it. So the opposite should also be true – if you think a stock is too expensive, you should sell it.

GMO UK Ltd strategist James Montier, has highlighted a study by Owen Lamont from Chicago University who has examined battles between companies and short sellers over a 25-year period. He looked at situations where a company had been 'attacked' by short sellers, and had then complained to the authorities, demanding that they investigate and tighten regulations. The performance of these companies was on average 24% worse than the market in the first year after the battle started, and 42% worse after three years. It appears that the short sellers did proper fundamental analysis, and the protests from management were in fact a red herring for bad business skills. If only long buyers did such rigorous research most people's pension funds might be in much better shape.

Be aware that all short selling, and especially naked short selling, is not without risk. In fact the risk is unlimited while the upside is only 100%, in other words a stock can only fall by 100%, but increases can be infinite (at least in theory!). I have had shorts in stock where the company tripled afterwards – this is why you have to use 'stops' at all times, as we will discuss later. If the market realises there is no merit to the negative rumours, and that short sellers have been active, prices will go up very fast (a short squeeze) leading to large losses for the short sellers.

By the way, the reverse is possible as well, where speculators buy into a certain stock (often penny or low-value stocks), and then spread false rumours about a possible takeover, causing the stock price to rally at which point 'innocent' investors are sold the shares. This all goes to show you should never believe what people tell you, and there is no substitute for doing the research yourself.

> **COMMON MISCONCEPTION:** Hedge fund
> managers want stocks to go down
>
> Contrary to what you may have read, hedge fund managers are
> not that different to other investors and do prefer markets to go
> up. Only a small number of hedge funds will actually make
> money when the market goes down; most just try to limit their
> losses by hedging their risk. Although it is obviously possible to
> profit from other people's misery it is pretty unlikely that you
> will make money when the world is falling apart around you.
>
> The reason stocks go down is not because of rumours
> generated by hedge fund managers, it is more likely because a
> business is being badly run, or the company is part of a sector
> that is being affected by wider economic turbulence. When a
> hedge fund manager is worried that his or her bank ('prime
> broker') might not be around tomorrow, they tend to be more
> concerned about maintaining their wealth than adding to it, just
> like you and me. The years 2008 and 2011 were terrible years
> for the stock market but also disastrous for many hedge funds
> with terrible overall performance and large redemptions. So I
> would say we can be fairly sure that hedge fund managers are
> not fans of falling markets.

▼ Exchange Traded Funds (ETFs)

Exchange Traded Funds were created to make it easier for
investors to trade more complicated instruments as if they were
a single stock. For example, if you want to trade commodities such
as wheat, sugar, oil or gold, for most people it is much easier to
trade them as stocks on the stock exchange, than it is to go to a
commodity exchange. That is why ETFs have been so successful
in recent years.

Alternatively, if you want to hedge your portfolio by selling the
FTSE 100 index, it is much more efficient to short one security

that tracks the FTSE 100 than a 100 single names, or than having to go to the futures exchange. If you don't think tracking the S&P 500 is exciting enough you can buy or sell a leveraged or 'turbo' version. You can also buy a currency ETF if you want to make a currency bet.

Recently there has been a lot of interest in gold as a hedge against a potential collapse of the financial system and to protect against governments printing large quantities of paper money and thereby fuelling inflation. However, it is difficult to buy and store gold in its physical form, and this is where a gold ETF comes in. All you would have to do is place an order as if it was a single stock.

In the case of a gold ETF it is important to realise that there is a company on the other side of the transaction that holds the gold in a vault. When you buy an ETF, you assume that the company is trustworthy, and will actually do what you have asked for. In theory, however, you should do research on the company that 'sponsors' the relevant ETF before you buy it.

▶ ▶ The inside track   ETFs

In September 2008 I was shocked that a number of agricultural ETFs, such as wheat and sugar, were suspended in London. I had assumed there were actual commodities behind these ETFs. In fact, these ETFs were guaranteed by American Insurance Group (AIG), something that might have seemed a good idea when this arrangement was made, but by September 2008 AIG was almost bankrupt.

If AIG had not been saved by the US government, your ETF could have ended up as a claim in the bankruptcy of AIG. Understanding risk in your portfolio involves questioning everything and everyone. You really can take nothing for granted.

▼ Investing overseas

This can often sound like a good idea, but there is one big drawback – the country must have a legal system that ensures that your property rights are respected.

Take Zimbabwe for example. This country does not have a good track record of protecting people's property. If you had been a local farmer in what was then called Southern Rhodesia, around 1900, you would have felt pretty wretched when the government

▷ Essential reading:

'The Age of Turbulence: Adventures in a New World', by Alan Greenspan

In this amazing book, Alan Greenspan describes his life and especially his experiences while he was chairman of the Federal Reserve of America between 1987 and 2006. Previously regarded as a hero, Greenspan has recently been criticised for letting the credit bubble develop on his watch. In this book he explains how he believes financial markets work, and what can and can't be expected from government. It will help you understand more about the powers and limitations of a central bank, a key player in global financial markets. His comments regarding property rights in overseas investments comprise one of his key observations, and I believe very few investors in emerging markets have taken notice, something that many have recently come to regret.

gave your land to white settlers. Equally, 100 years later, white farmers were outraged when a very different government took the land back. Any country where land ownership is subject to the whim of government is not a good investment prospect.

▼ Ponzi schemes

The career of a man called Charles Ponzi provides a good illustration of why it pays to be street smart and not too greedy in the world of trading and investing.

Ponzi emigrated to the US from Italy at the beginning of the 20th century. He had a great investment proposition, which involved buying local postal stamps at a low price in Italy, taking advantage of a US law that would allow them to be changed without an additional charge for a higher-priced local stamp in the US. This was an early form of what we now call risk arbitrage: buying the same asset cheap in one place and selling it at a higher price elsewhere.

Ponzi was very good at selling his scheme and promised investors unusually high returns. As lots of money came into his company from eager investors he was not able to generate the returns he promised. He reassured existing investors that their money was safe, but was paying those leaving the scheme with money that was coming in from new investors, rather than with money that was legitimately earned through his postal arbitrage. In the end the investors lost everything.

Risk arbitrage

The practice of buying the same asset cheap in one place and selling it at a higher price elsewhere.

In December 2008 Bernard Madoff was running a strategy where he invested in blue chip companies and enhanced returns with a relatively simple derivatives strategy. The return he claimed to have made from 1990 to 2008 can be seen below.

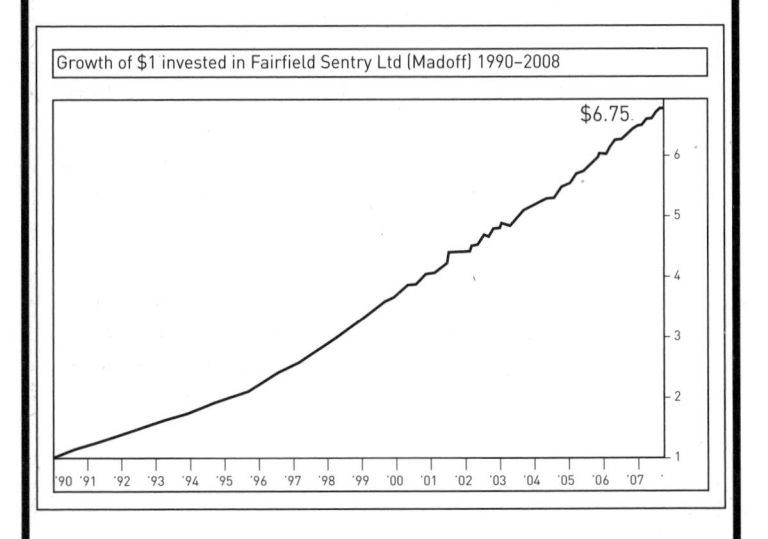

Growth of $1 invested in Fairfield Sentry Ltd (Madoff) 1990–2008

A few years ago I was asked if I would recommend investing in one of the Madoff funds. I looked at a similar chart to the one above, and told the would-be investor that it looked too good to be true. Luckily he listened to me. The amazing thing about this chart was that it only went up – there were no down months at all. No one quite understood how his strategy could make such high and consistent returns.

Later it was revealed that during the past 13 years, Madoff executed no trades at all. The apparent growth in his fund simply represented money coming in from investors; few people were withdrawing money as most were happy with their paper statements, which showed healthy returns. Retail and professional investors alike were clamouring to be part of Madoff's fund.

Ironically, professional investors (and especially the fund of hedge funds, whose sole reason for existence is their expertise in building a portfolio of different hedge funds on behalf of their clients) pride themselves on their due diligence – in fact it is their main selling point. They usually ask the funds they invest in hundreds of questions about their strategy, but in the case of Madoff, either they did not ask the right questions, or they did not check the answers – it probably just seemed too good an opportunity to miss.

Madoff did not lose money for everyone. The salespeople who sold his funds earned very high commission rates. However, they are now subject to legal action from those who lost money.

There are three big lessons here:

1. Avoid investments that look too good to be true – Madoff's is by no means the only Ponzi scheme around.

2. Check the commission rates of the salespeople that are trying to sell to you. You could even try asking the salesperson if he or she would be happy to refund you their commission in case of you losing money.

3. If you ever consider investing in a fund of hedge funds, make sure they did not invest with Madoff before you part with your money.

Names to know: JP Morgan

John Pierpont (JP) Morgan (1837–1913) was the son of a successful financier called Junius Spencer Morgan, and is probably the best-known name in banking. He is said to have saved the US financial system from collapsing on several occasions by acting as the leader of the financial industry. He was also the architect of what was once the biggest company in the world, General Electric, through the merger of Edison General Electric and Thompson-Houston, and the formation of the United States Steel Corp. in 1902.

He was a board member for many corporations and almost all the railway companies. Morgan helped restructure the railways by taking initial control, reducing their debt, and appointing key people he could trust to manage the companies. At a time when reliance upon railways was growing, he controlled over 5,000 miles of railroads helping to increase his wealth and influence. Morgan, along with great 'robber barons', such as Cornelius Vanderbilt and John D. Rockefeller, believed that too much competition within markets only led to waste and losses, and felt increased consolidation led to increased efficiency.

Morgan went on to gain control of a vast group of banks and insurance companies, and it was his financial influence that allowed him achieve one of his greatest feats – preventing a run on the banks during the Panic of 1907. During this crisis of confidence, he organised a group of leading bankers to pool together enough funds to rescue any banks in crisis, and thereby successfully prevented a systemic banking crisis. The bank he created became so powerful that in 1933 it was broken up to separate its investment banking activities from its commercial banking. The investment bank Morgan Stanley was born. The overseas activities were spun-off under the name Morgan Grenfell. The rest would later again use the very valuable brand name J.P. Morgan & Co.

▶What can we learn from the City?

I realise that my view of finance and the City is a cynical one. My aim is to encourage you to be sceptical of so-called 'experts' and do the work yourself. Within my investment framework I will explain how important it is to build your own view of the world and that you invest with that in mind. You must also understand how the rest of the world looks at things so that you can see whether your opinion is different. For instance, if you take a negative view on house builders in the early part of a recession, that may or may not be an original idea or a good trading idea. But if you learn to look at the world from a trader's perspective, there will be no need to give your money to someone who will make those decisions for you – why put your future in the hands of a stranger who is unlikely to have your best interests at heart?

> IF WE BECOME INCREASINGLY
> HUMBLE ABOUT HOW LITTLE WE KNOW.
> WE MAY BE MORE EAGER TO SEARCH.

JOHN TEMPLETON

> Chapter 2

The framework for trading

As soon as you start to trade you are putting your money at risk. This chapter outlines the steps I think you should take before you make a new investment.

Trading is what I have been doing for a living for the last 19 years. I have had a variety of trading related jobs and each one has helped me hone my techniques. Some of the key skills I developed and the thoughts that helped me focus at different stages are outlined below.

Company	Key thoughts	Key skills
Goldman Sachs Trading client orders UK shares	'It is the buyers and sellers who set the price, not the person who is theoretically right' 'The market can remain irrational longer than you can remain solvent'	▷ Knowing companies inside out ▷ Understanding charts ▷ Being on top of (economic) news flow in UK and abroad ▷ Knowing opinions of analysts ▷ Understanding the flow of money
Goldman Sachs Proprietary trading European shares and derivatives	'You need to develop a consistent trading strategy'	▷ Developing risk strategies: don't lose too much money, build up business slowly ▷ Patience – the market will always be around
GLG Hedge fund manager European shares and derivatives	'You need to have the courage to follow your own opinions'	▷ Balancing client demands with successful trading ▷ Learning that being right is not the same as making money ▷ Understanding that investors do not always know what is good for them
Lex Van Dam Trading Academy lexvandam.com	'Teaching professional methods of trading'	▷ 5-Step-Trading ®

Company	Key thoughts	Key skills
Hampstead Capital Hedge fund manager	'It is a long term game'	▷ Realising you need to have the same personal objectives as your clients
Global shares and derivatives		▷ It's all about preservation of capital

Chapter 2 represents the accumulated wisdom of my trading experiences and trading knowledge. It is designed to show you the different steps you take, and the issues you encounter when investing and building a portfolio.

There are eight areas you need to consider each and every time you put on a new trade:

1. Understanding the world and the investment environment
Getting a handle on this can help you establish a framework for your investments. Without it you will be trading in the dark.

2. What we can learn from the past
Understanding past events will help you make more informed decisions. Without this you might try to reinvent the wheel.

3. Idea generation
Ideas are crucial to making good investments so you need to know how and where to find them.

4. Analysing companies
It is important to know how to look at companies: what is current business like? How capable is management? Just make sure you don't get seduced by management and fall in love with a company.

5. Analysing stock movements
Interpreting data is an essential skill for a trader. Charts show how stock prices have developed over time and reading these correctly will help you make the right decisions.

6. Reality check
Steps 1–5 are designed to help you make better investment decisions; now you need to combine this with some street smarts.

7. Head check
Ask yourself the question 'Am I ready to trade (today)?' If not wait till you are mentally able to do it. You need to be focused and able to cope with losses when trading.

8. Building your portfolio and controlling its risks
Discipline is everything when trading. Every decision must be based on risk and return, and when you do trade you need to have a plan about what to do when your assessments turn out to be wrong, i.e. when to 'cut' your position and accept your losses.

When you have gone through these eight stages you are ready to put on the trade. If things don't quite add up forget about the trade (at least for now) and start again. Learn to trust yourself. Don't forget to look at all these variables every day: you need to ensure your portfolio is a current one – trading is clearly not for the lazy. If you don't quite remember why you have a certain stock position, don't worry – just get rid of it. The chances are that you will start losing money if you don't. Once again, good luck!

▶Part 1

Understanding the world and the investment environment

When building my investment framework the first and perhaps the single most important question to ask is 'What kind of market am I in?'

▼ Bull and bear markets

It sounds simple but more often than not people forget that there are essentially two different types of investment environment: bull and bear markets.

As the investment game is all about probabilities you really want the probability of your trade being right to be higher than 50:50. Thus, if you are long (i.e. you own equities) in a bull market you will more likely make money than if you are short (i.e. have sold equities in the hope of buying them back at lower prices). The reverse applies too for bear markets; you will tend to make money in a bear market if you are short.

Bull market

A market where prices tend to rise and investors feel good about investing in stocks.

Bear market

There are different ways to describe a bear market. One commonly used definition is that when a market is trading 20% below its previous highest level, it has entered a bear market. It also tends to be a period characterised by rising unemployment and widespread pessimism.

▷ Market bias

Unfortunately future market direction is not always crystal clear, and people have a tendency towards a bias in their view, regardless of what the market is doing. This is true of vastly experienced professional investors as well as novices. Most people have a long bias: when a bear market occurs they generally expect to return quickly to the previous bull market. This is why people so often lose money in a bear market. A deeply ingrained bias like this means you will lose money, so it is important to learn to trade with the trend in your favour.

Clearly, at market turning points it is often very hard to predict what the market direction will be at first, but over time things will become more obvious. Don't trade without hedging yourself if you don't know what the market direction is. Later we will discuss tools to help you make an informed decision about market direction using economic, fundamental and technical analysis.

▷ Current market conditions

Looking at a chart of the current FTSE 100, it is clear that over the past year we have been trading in a range between 5000 and 6000, and we are currently exactly in the middle of this range.

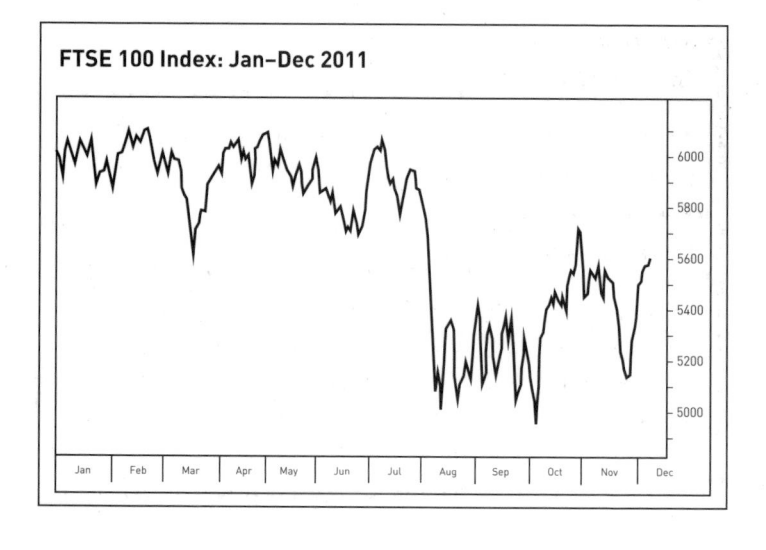

FTSE 100 Index: Jan–Dec 2011

▷ Investment time horizon

However, when you take into account your investment time horizon things start to get a little more complicated as seen in the chart below.

If you are a longer-term trader you can see two clear trends:

1. A downtrend from late 2007 to early 2009.
2. An uptrend from early 2009 to the middle of 2011.

But as the chart on p.49 shows, we are currently in a ranging market and the preferred strategy would be to buy the lower end of the range and sell the higher end of the range until we convincingly break out above 6000 or break down below 5000.

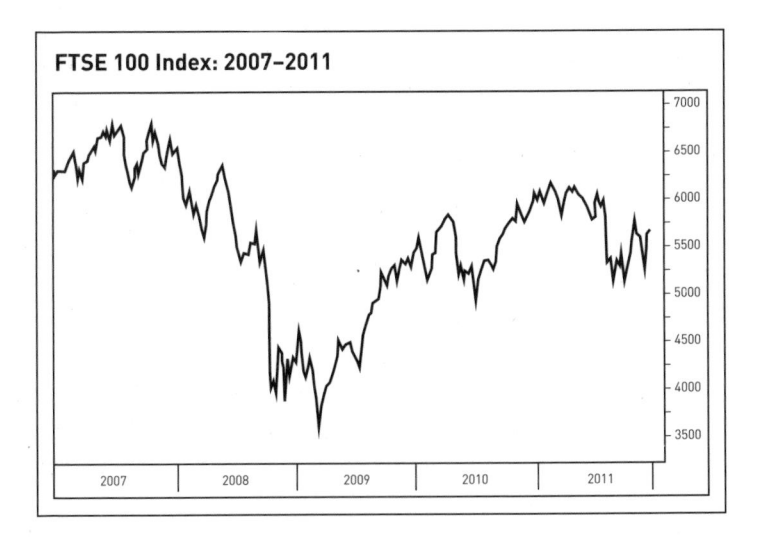

FTSE 100 Index: 2007–2011

Investment time horizon

The length of time over which an investment is made or held before it is liquidated.

What has always surprised me is the number of investment professionals and so-called 'experts' who, in the midst of the recent financial crisis and the resulting bear market – the biggest for over 50 years – have been calling for investors to buy stocks in anticipation of the next rally. They did this when the FTSE was 6500, 5500, 4500, 3500, and of course they will be right at some point ...

A clever trader would resist catching this 'falling knife' and remain biased towards short side investments. You should make the decision as to whether the trend has turned or is likely to turn on your own – you cannot trust anyone else to do this for you. You only need a few tools to be able to do this as well as, if not better than, an average strategist or economist.

▷ Secular trends

The very hardest markets are those in a secular (extremely long-term) trend where the counter-trend moves can be huge. These can be incredibly rewarding if you understand what kind of market you are in or can destroy your capital very quickly if you do not. There are two prime examples.

The first is the bear market in Japanese shares after the stock market bubble burst in 1990. As you can see from the chart below, the market in Japan has fallen over 75% over the 21 years since

Secular trends

Extremely long term stock market trends either upwards or downwards.

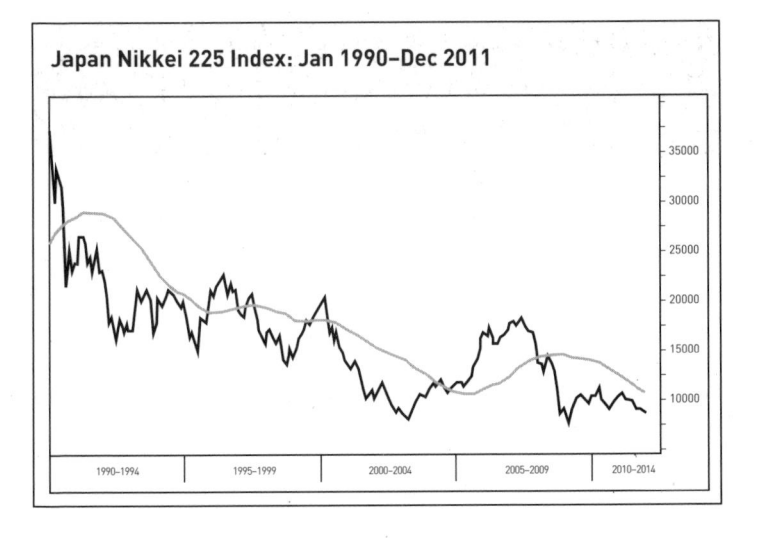

Japan Nikkei 225 Index: Jan 1990–Dec 2011

then, but the decline has been interspersed with rallies that have lasted for a year or more. In this event, every rally was a selling opportunity.

The second prime example and the opposite of the secular bear market in Japan, was the secular bull market in the US stock

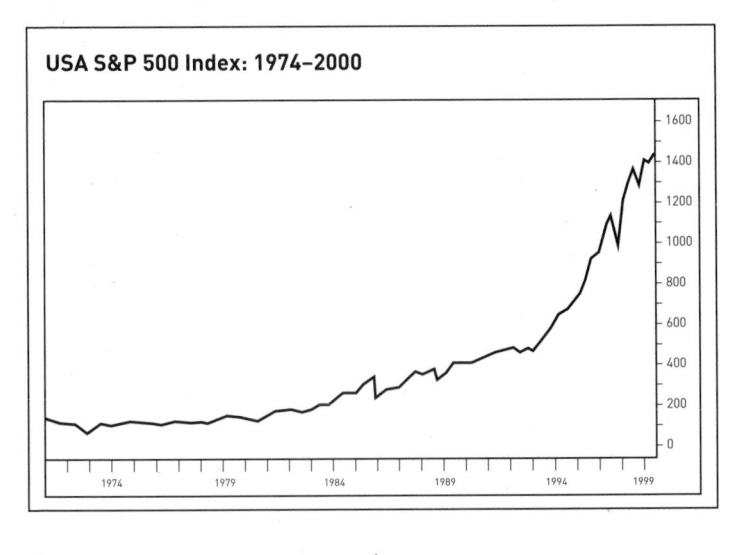

USA S&P 500 Index: 1974–2000

REMEMBER:
THE TREND IS YOUR FRIEND.

market between 1974 and 2000 (see above). In this case, every sell off was a buying opportunity, including the horrific stock market crash of 1987, which now looks like a small blip on the chart. The key to understanding secular markets is having a good grasp of history and the business cycle. Understanding the business cycle will also help you identify at what stage you are at in a normal bull or bear market.

COMMON MISCONCEPTION: Bad news for a company means its stock price falls

The stock market is a village with many inhabitants. These inhabitants have a huge interest in staying on top of the latest news stories and gossip, because they know all the old stories, and only what is different to yesterday really matters. They know which companies are the higher quality ones and which ones have a lot of debt on their balance sheet. If a new inhabitant arrives in the village, he might see a company and think that it is in a sector that has no future, and is run by an incompetent management team. His instinct tells him to short this company; however the market is a great discount mechanism for all news that is already in the public domain and all that matters is expectations versus reality. Bad news does not matter if the market players have already priced it into the stock. For example, if a company reports a loss of £100 million, this looks negative by most measures, but if the market was expecting a loss of £200 million the stock might rally hard. So if you want to trade profitably you need to know what other people are thinking first.

▼ The business cycle

A general understanding of economics will help you tremendously when trying to make money. You certainly don't need to be an economist to predict or at least understand where we are in the business cycle.

Why is this so important? The answer is because the business cycle is the key driver of investment returns and is what creates bull and bear markets.

Let's take a closer look at what the business cycle actually is. Don't get too bogged down in dictionary definitions – economists have fought over these for decades. All you need to know is that the economy has a tendency to expand and contract in a relatively predictable way over time.

Business cycle

The tendency of economies to move through periods of boom and bust, with fluctuations in economic growth occurring every five years or so.

▷ Gross Domestic Product (GDP)

GDP can be used as a measure of whether the economy is expanding or contracting. The chart below shows GDP annual growth since 1956, and as you can see it has fluctuated a great deal over time. These oscillations are an indication of the business cycle, which is effectively a measure of how the economy is doing.

> ECONOMICS IS NO SCIENCE
> REGARDLESS OF WHAT PEOPLE
> TELL YOU IT IS MORE OF AN ART.

Gross Domestic Product

Gross Domestic Product or GDP is the monetary value of all goods and services produced by an economy over a specified period.

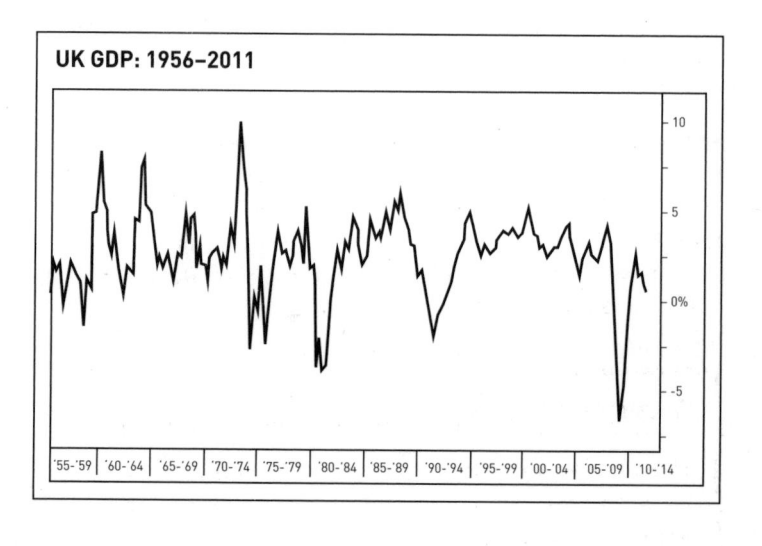

UK GDP: 1956–2011

▷ Economic growth

If you look at the chart above you can see that economic growth in the UK is around 3% on average. This is referred to as the trend rate of growth. In strong periods of growth the economy can peak at much higher rates of growth and in recessions economic growth will fall below zero.

As a rule , economies with strong rates of growth produce strong profits and thus strong stock markets, and in periods of recession tend to produce weak profits and share prices fall.

Just to keep it simple for now, we can see that the last four UK recessions occurred in 2008–09, 1989–90, 1979–80 and 1972–74. During those recessions the stock market fell in all instances. Between 1972 and 1974 the UK market fell 71%, in 1979 to 1980 the market fell around 20%, in 1989 to 1990 the market fell around 25%, and at the lows in 2009 the market had fallen 48% from its 2007 highs.

▷ The economy of the US is key

However, don't fall into the trap of using changes in the UK economy exclusively to track UK share prices, and the reason for this is that there is one giant economy that affects markets throughout the world, and that is the United States.

The single most important thing you can do for your investment framework is to understand what the US economy is doing – the US economy drives the UK economy. Take a look at this chart of UK GDP against US GDP ... they are pretty much the same.

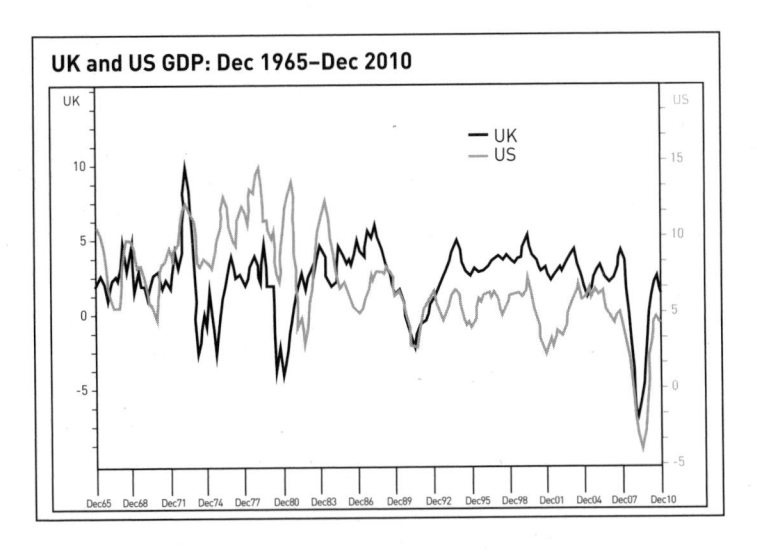

UK and US GDP: Dec 1965–Dec 2010

If we therefore use the US economy as our framework we need to learn how to predict US GDP.

▷ The ISM Survey

The single best tool for predicting US GDP is to understand something called the Institute for Supply Management Manufacturers Survey (ISM). Effectively it is a survey that asks the purchasing managers of major businesses a series of questions about the economic climate. This may sound vague, but the data is put together in an index, which has been published since 1947. This index gives us a tremendous amount of data to use and if you compare it to GDP you can see it is an extremely good lead indicator.

You can find the ISM survey on www.ism.ws. It not only gives a number, which is used in our charts, but also a summary of the current state of affairs in the economy. In November 2011 it said 'Economic activity in the manufacturing sector expanded in November for the 28th consecutive month, and the overall economy grew for the 30th consecutive month'. This does not sound too bad!

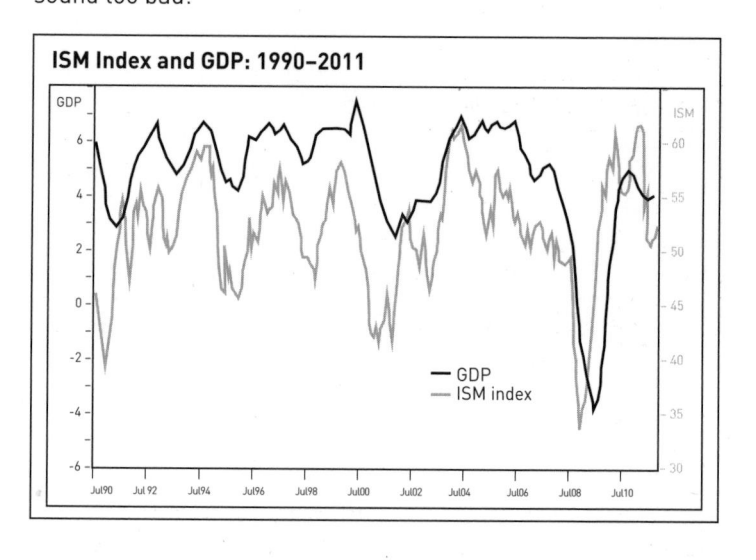

ISM Index and GDP: 1990–2011

What do I mean by lead indicator? Well the ISM moves in cycles in the same way as GDP and it usually leads GDP by several months. That helps us predict changes in GDP. The ISM almost always oscillates from its peak to a trough below 50 indicating a recession is imminent. If you remember, the chart of GDP seemed to do the same, as it moves from its peak to its trough below zero. When the ISM is above 50 the economy is expanding, and when it is below 50 the economy will soon start to contract, or is contracting already. And as mentioned above, the business cycle is just that – the tendency for an economy to go from strength to weakness and back again.

When someone asks you what you think the economy is going to do over the next few years you can look at the ISM. If it peaked a while ago and is heading towards 50 then you can say with near certainty that the economy is going to either slow down or go into recession in the next 18 months to 2 years.

The ISM has only given two false signals since 1947 (i.e. in those instances a recession did not follow after the ISM peaked out at the top of the cycle). This occurred in 1994 and 1967. In those years the ISM peaked and rolled over but the trough did not equate to a recession. However, in every other instance since 1947 it has worked. These are extremely good odds and makes the ISM a very valuable tool indeed.

I am amazed that so many economists failed to see the last recession coming. The ISM peaked in 2004, which suggested that the economy was going to get weaker rather than stronger – and that is exactly what happened. Most economists expected the

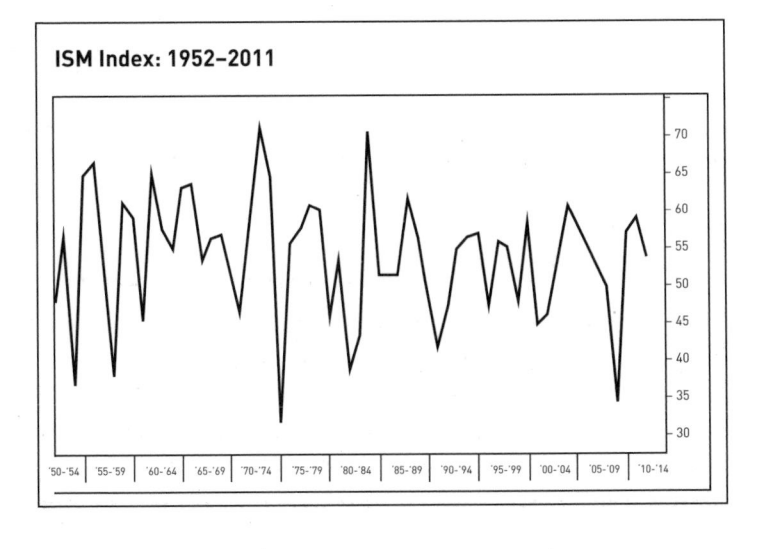

ISM Index: 1952–2011

good times to go on forever, but even a cursory glance shows us that the good times never go on forever, and the business cycle always moves from peak to trough over time.

If, as can be seen on the chart below, you now overlay equity price moves on the ISM chart, you can see that they are a pretty good fit. The health of US businesses drives US stock prices, and those of almost all countries in the world. The year on year return of equities almost exactly matches that of the business cycle ...

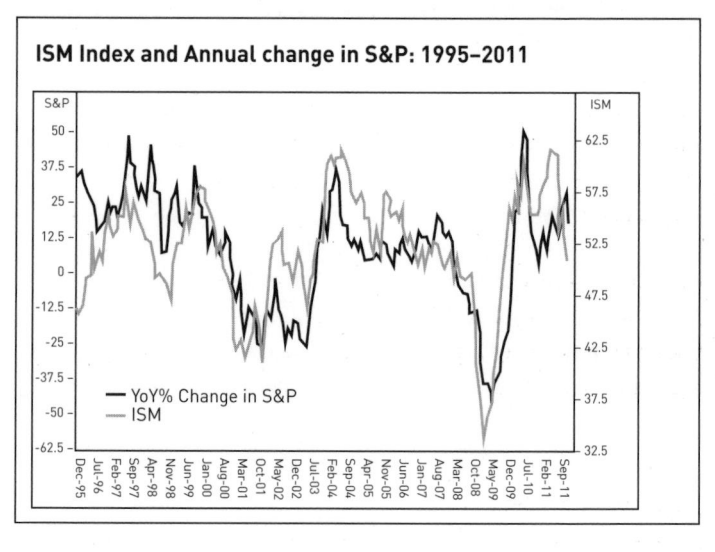

ISM Index and Annual change in S&P: 1995–2011

And it even works for Asian stock markets. People remained too bullish of Asian equities, even when all the evidence pointed to

Cyclicals

Basic resources, such as oil and copper, that perform well in the markets during upturns as the economy expands, but do badly in downturns as manufacturing capacity contracts. That is why these sectors are often called 'cyclicals': they move with the business cycle.

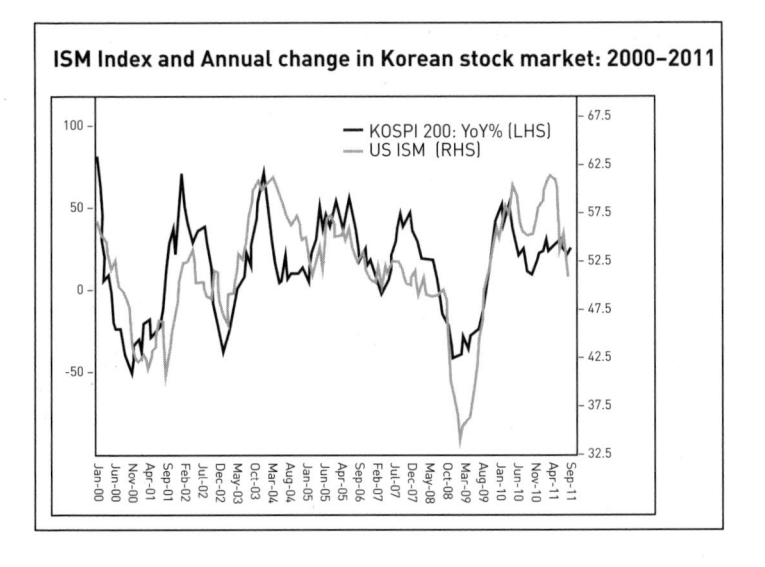

ISM Index and Annual change in Korean stock market: 2000–2011

— KOSPI 200: YoY% (LHS)
— US ISM (RHS)

them falling along with the US economy. See the chart of the Korean Kospi Index of shares versus ISM (above).

What is even more useful is that the ISM survey also perfectly predicts returns in other asset classes, such as oil, copper or bonds. That not only helps us when investing in these assets, but also helps us to understand how related stock market sectors, such as mining, are going to perform.

This is also true of consumer goods such as cars or designer clothes. When the economy is weak people buy less of them. Makes sense doesn't it? Economics can be pretty useful!

▼ Taking a view

By now it should be clear that it is not that difficult to have a view on the economy, and to make a basic prediction about the future of equity markets, or even the sub-sectors.

People spend far too long worrying about inflation and deflation and all the other elements of economic analysis, when the ISM Survey encapsulates it all, and does a great job in helping you make money. However, we cannot follow one indicator in isolation;

it needs to be added to our mix, alongside all the other aspects of our analysis. The key to becoming really proficient is knowing when you are making predictions that have a high chance of being correct, but that go against the market consensus, and thus give you great odds. Getting to that stage takes a lot of practice.

COMMON MISCONCEPTION: Reading the paper and watching financial news channels will make you money

There are many journalists who specialise in reporting and writing about stocks and the stock market. Most of them are very knowledgeable – often more so than people who actually trade stocks. However, when news shows up in the paper it tends to be yesterday's news. The market has already seen this news and it has been priced into the stock. If there was great news about a company's earnings yesterday, the stock might well have gone up already, and if it did not there are probably good reasons for it. I am not saying you should not read the paper – you should, as it will show you what all the other market participants are looking at, and it will help you generate ideas – but in itself it will not make you any money. Your job is to 'predict' tomorrow's newspaper!

Financial news channels also have very smart and capable journalists and presenters. However, once again they tend to focus on the latest news and the latest interests of their audience. Their main aim is to attract viewers, which is not necessarily the same as making their viewers money. These channels often feature guests with very strong views, and these guests have been chosen because they make good television, and are prepared to discuss their views in front of hundreds of thousands of viewers. The traders I rate and whom I know personally would never go on television to talk about their opinions on the market – they are way too busy investing and tend to keep their views private. This is not to say that I don't rate any of the guests that appear, they are just few and far between.

My biggest issue is that those featured never seem to admit that they were wrong the last time they were on the same channel. They might tell you that you should buy particular stocks and make a very convincing case. However, they probably made the same case when these stocks were 50% higher, and had you listened to them you would have lost a third of your money! So watch for entertainment but don't expect it to make you money.

THE AVERAGE MAN DOESN'T WISH TO BE TOLD THAT IT IS A BULL OR A BEAR MARKET. WHAT HE DESIRES IS TO BE TOLD SPECIFICALLY WHICH PARTICULAR STOCK TO BUY OR SELL. HE WANTS TO GET SOMETHING FOR NOTHING. HE DOES NOT WISH TO WORK. HE DOESN'T EVEN WISH TO HAVE TO THINK.

JESSE LIVERMORE

►Part 2

What we can learn from the past

I believe it is crucial for anyone who invests in markets to have a decent understanding of economic and stock market history. Economics was covered in the previous section, and we will now have a look at stock market history. I don't just mean facts and dates, but an overall understanding of key market events, and why they occurred. If you have a genuine interest in trading you will probably find it interesting, and it will really help you to understand the current environment better, and what might happen in the future.

I find the lazy economic analysis of many so-called 'experts' extremely frustrating: they look at the last 10–20 years and use this data to draw conclusions about the present day. In fact, this type of analysis is next to useless, as the last two decades have been about as far removed from the norm as at any time over the last 200 years!

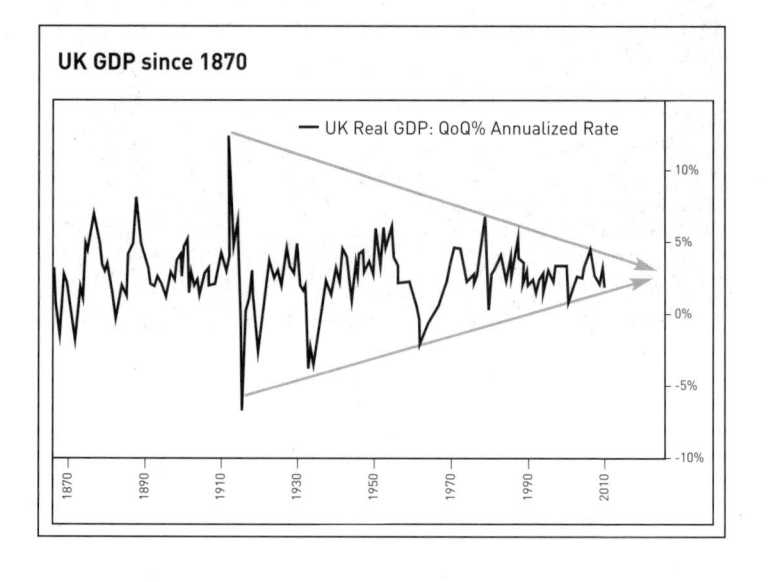

UK GDP since 1870

▼ Economic history

The first thing you need is a chart showing UK GDP over time. This illustrates the extent of previous fluctuations in the economy, and what normal expansions and recessions look like.

The chart on the previous page shows the pattern of previous recessions, when GDP contracted to below zero, and periods of economic expansion. It gives an idea of how bad recessions can be and how long they usually last. It also shows clearly that the post-WWII period has seen a relatively benign business cycle with lower peaks and troughs, but as I mentioned before, this is certainly not the norm.

▼ Stock market history

Second, you need to see a long-term chart of the stock market, and familiarize yourself with the various major bull and bear markets, and cross reference that with the economy at the time (using the GDP charts). That will help you predict how big the moves may be within the stock market. You can see clearly that big recessions cause big stock market declines and big booms cause big equity bull markets.

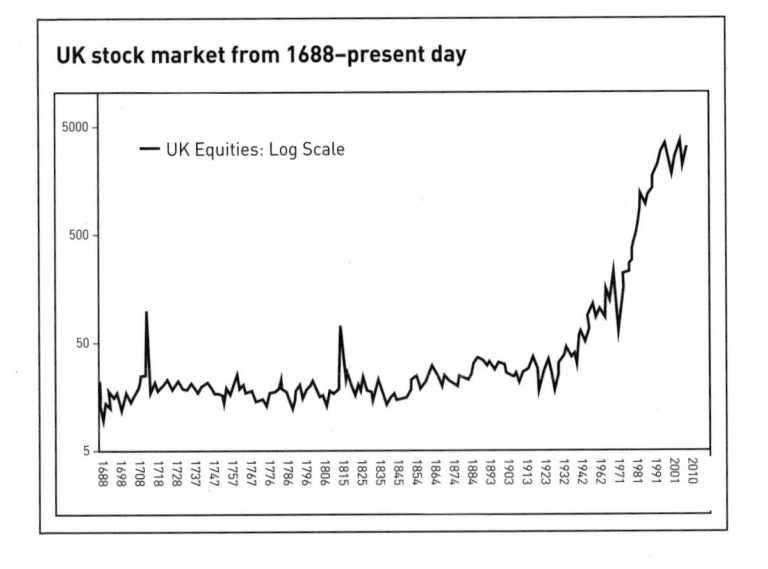

UK stock market from 1688–present day

— UK Equities: Log Scale

Notice how stocks have now finished one of their biggest runs in the history of the UK equity market – this is the only such bull market that spanned several generations. Prior to that, between the 1690s and the 1960s, the market traded in a wide sideways range. Huge booms seem to be the exception and not the rule.

▼ Starting points

Third, you need to understand that experts may not tell you the whole truth. Many people will tell you that stocks go up 6–8% in the long run, but in reality the only thing we can predict in the long run, is that we will all be dead! But more importantly, this data is not strictly accurate because it depends on your starting point.

For example, if you take as the starting point the trough in the US equity market in 1933, you will show very good returns, as this was the lowest point in a long time. However, if you took 1929 as your starting point, then it would have taken until 1954 for American stocks actually to produce a positive return.

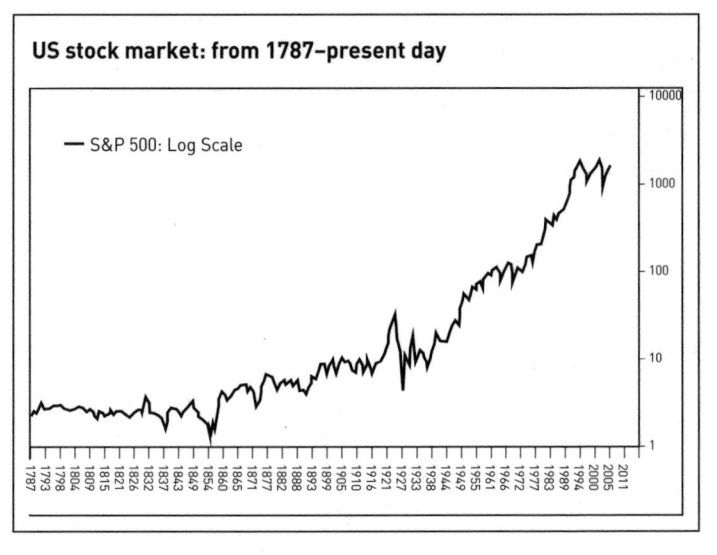

US stock market: from 1787–present day

— S&P 500: Log Scale

Using the long-term average of the UK stock market we can see that it has produced average annual returns of just 1.34% – not a great investment.

▼ Historical valuations

In order to make a judgement about when is a good time to buy, we also need to learn about historical valuations. Generally, studies show that expensive stock markets, valued using either dividend yields (low dividend yield means expensive market) or Price Earnings ratios (high P/E ratio means expensive market, see p.88), often produce below par returns over the next decade or so, while cheap markets usually produce strong returns. Therefore we must know the long-term history of the valuation of equities, and where we are now. Most market experts use too little history, and therefore make inadequate predictions.

Starting at the simplest level, looking at the 10-year average of P/Es (to make it a smoother line), we can easily see the huge swings in valuations in the stock market. Markets tend to get very over-valued in major bull markets and very undervalued in major bear markets. Notice how expensive the market became by 2000. It also shows that the market is still not back to its average valuation over the long term, and as you can see from the chart, usually a major bear market will bring valuations down to cheaper levels. Using a chart of dividend yields to assess valuations would give us a similar conclusion: i.e. equities are still not that cheap.

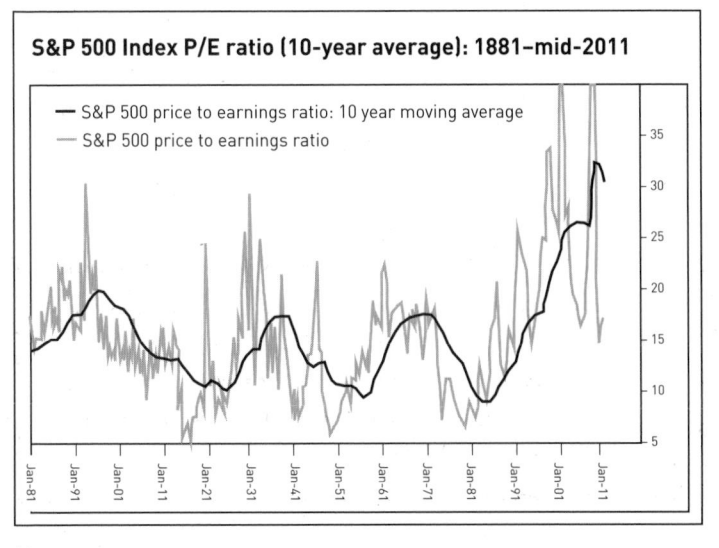

S&P 500 Index P/E ratio (10-year average): 1881–mid-2011

— S&P 500 price to earnings ratio: 10 year moving average
— S&P 500 price to earnings ratio

Price to earnings ratio (P/E)

Stock price divided by earnings per share. The higher the P/E the more expensive a company.

▶Stock market bubbles

Throughout history financial markets experienced bubbles, where buyers scramble to get hold of scarce assets, and push prices to unsustainable levels, only to see them crashing down afterwards. According to top investor George Soros: 'Stock market bubbles don't grow out of thin air. They have a solid basis in reality, but reality as distorted by a misconception.' In a bubble investors believe that it is easy to make money out of nothing. The ironic thing is, that a lot of people know that these situations are bubbles all along, but cannot resist participating. The rationale is that as long as there is another investor prepared to pay more, why not buy now, and sell to that investor tomorrow. Unfortunately the bubble always bursts, and what was worth a fortune yesterday, is worth pennies today.

The invention of the car is one example of where a revolutionary technology was misinterpreted as a great investment opportunity. Thousands of car companies appeared at the beginning of the 20th century and they seemed great investments to the people

Stock market bubble

A period of stock market euphoria where stocks trade at ever-higher prices, becoming more and more detached from the underlying economic reality. Every stock market bubble ends in tears, unfortunately the timing of this is almost impossible to predict.

▶ ▶ The inside track
The Internet bubble

When people bought Internet stocks in the late 1990s, without caring too much about the underlying economics, the common rationale was that the Internet would fundamentally change the way the world would do business. It would lower transaction costs and be enormously profitable for the companies that were involved. The industry was able to attract the best talent in the world, and many an investment banker left a secure job to join Internet start-ups. It was a period during which it seemed that any company that was remotely related to the Internet was able to raise a huge amount of capital. When a new Internet company was listed on the stock market it was not uncommon for the stock to double or triple on the first day of trading.

Most fund managers, although often sceptical, were not able to resist getting involved. They were forced to buy these stocks, as not owning them would not be an easy sell to their clients.

Graph showing Internet index DOT 1998–2001

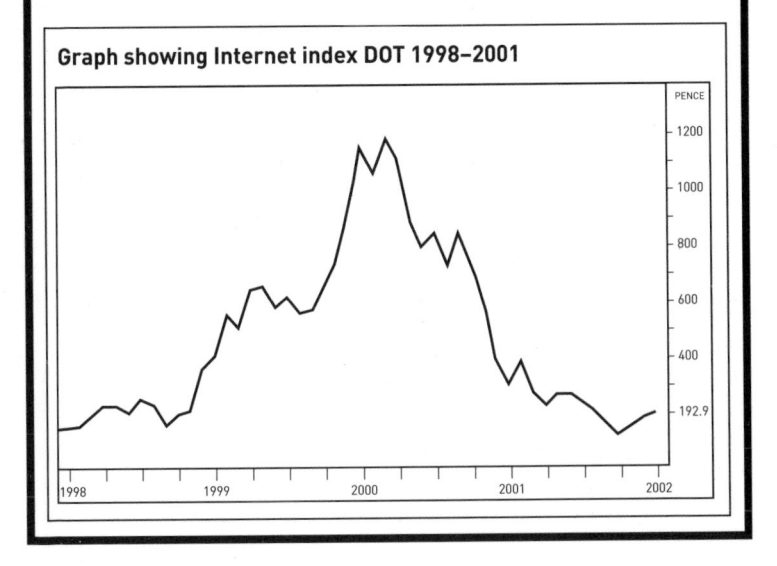

What a lot of people did not realise is that the existence of a new technology that was going to change their lives does not mean that the companies who deliver this technology will necessarily be profitable investments.

Easynet Group PLC share price Dec 1996–Dec 2005

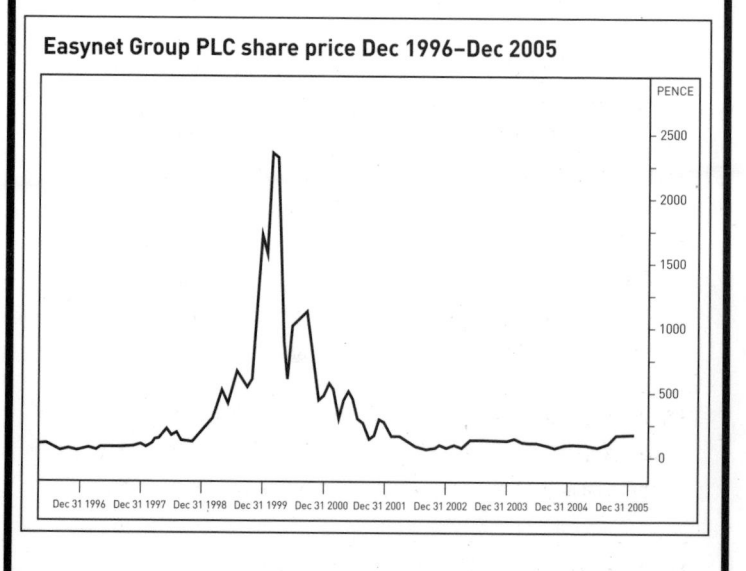

Easynet Group PLC was a company that provided Internet access. Its share price took off like a rocket when the world went Internet mad and collapsed when the frenzy died down (see chart above). It was an outperformer versus most, however, and in 2006 it was bought by BskyB, at a fraction of the maximum stock price it had reached before.

who bought the shares at ever higher levels. The car did change the world, but very few car companies were able to make money, and in the end stock prices reverted to underlying economic reality, i.e. a disaster. Even the largest of them all, General Motors, has gone bankrupt and is now controlled by the US government. More recently we have seen the Internet bubble with only a handful of companies turning out to be great investments (so far), such as Amazon, eBay and Google.

Let's use a topical example. We all know we are running out of oil, and alternative energy sources are a technology that will change the world. But do you really think you will make money out of wind power and solar energy? My bet is that you won't.

The 1999 book *Dow 36,000*, was written at a time when the Dow Jones Index was around 10,000. According to the authors, it would soon reach 36,000. The Dow Jones had been just 5,000 three years earlier, so had already undergone a 100% rally in a few years. The book said that all traditional valuation measures were out of date and that a new era had arrived. In 2012 the Dow Jones is trading just over 12,000, having traded under 7,000 in 2009. Things are never different. Markets are the result of human behaviour and people never learn. Human greed is infectious and we must resist getting involved in investing during stock market bubbles. Why take the risk?

It is also important to be able to distinguish between a stock market bubble and a broad financial crisis. When the Internet bubble burst in 2000 it did not cause a real financial crisis; certainly many people lost a lot of money, but the world economy did not shrink. In fact interest rates were lowered, and stocks soon resumed their upward path.

GREAT INVENTIONS DO NOT OFTEN MAKE GOOD INVESTMENTS.

▼ History: a valuable lesson

If you look back and put together what you now know about economic, stock market and valuation history, you can see that the best possible time to buy equities was after the recession in 1981. At this point the bear market was ending but market valuation was still low. It also shows you clearly that 2000, the peak of the Internet bubble, was the single worst time in history to buy equities!

The key incentive for understanding history, is that you will be better able to make informed decisions yourself, and rely less on the often-biased research produced by those within the financial industry. So the next time you hear someone on television, or read an article in the newspaper telling you that stocks are cheap, you will know not blindly to believe them.

Now that you understand the importance of economics and stock market history, we can move onto step three of our investment process: how to generate ideas.

COMMON MISCONCEPTION:
Stocks go up in the long term

I don't think so. Most companies have a life cycle just like you and me: they start small and they end up small. Most companies never become remotely large, but the ones that do are the ones we know about. There is a definite 'winners bias' in our heads. Our minds are focused on a few companies that have been around 'forever' and will continue to be around 'forever'. In fact, nothing lasts forever.

The charts below belong to two UK banks: Northern Rock and Bradford & Bingley. How many financial advisers told their clients to sell these stocks before it was too late?

Northern Rock: 2004–2008

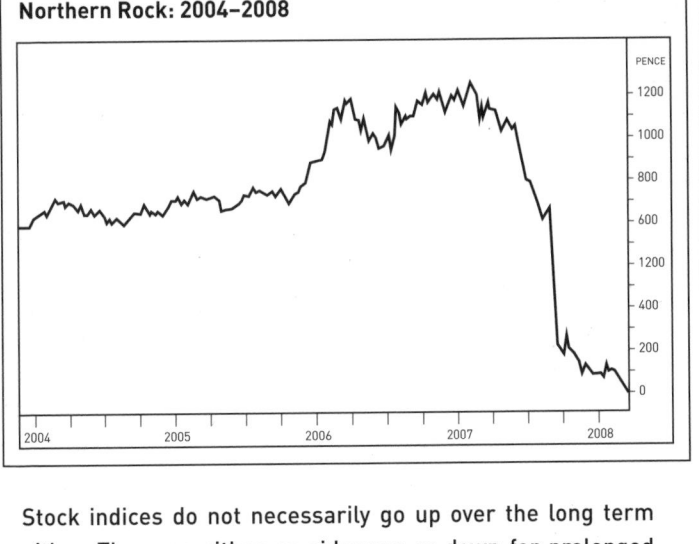

Stock indices do not necessarily go up over the long term either. They can either go sideways or down for prolonged periods of time, as we saw earlier in the UK stock chart, where stocks went sideways from 1690 until 1960.

Bradford & Bingley: 2004–2008

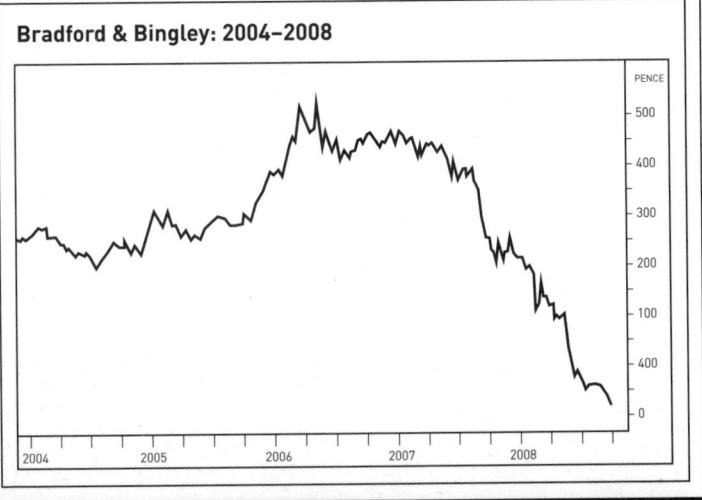

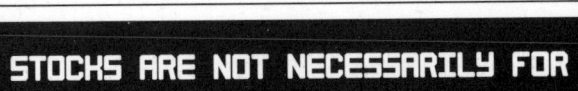

STOCKS ARE NOT NECESSARILY FOR THE LONG RUN.

► Part 3

Idea generation

This is where the real work begins. You cannot undertake any of the subsequent (technical or fundamental) analysis if you do not know what stocks you should be looking at, and you cannot build a portfolio if you have no ideas of your own.

Generating ideas takes time and experience. To be good at it you need to start following the news and the markets. It is important to read newspapers and see how stocks react to news events. What you will find is often counter intuitive. A company can have excellent results but still sell off (i.e. the stock price still goes down). It may be that the market had anticipated these good results and the stock had already rallied before the results were published. If that same company had actually had bad results that could have been a total disaster for the stock price as it would have been completely unexpected. Another stock might report bad results and nobody seems to care. Or, one day the oil price goes up and oil stocks sell off with the market and the next day oil goes up again but this time oil stocks rally.

The apparently inconsistent behaviour of the stock market can be very frustrating. That is also why the best way to start is by trading small positions. Do not trade without doing the work and do not trade too frequently. There is no rush, you can trade for the rest of your life if you are careful, respect risk and stay disciplined.

> 'IF I GET AN IDEA NEXT WEEK.
> I'LL DO SOMETHING.
> IF NOT. I WON'T DO A DAMN THING'.
>
> WARREN BUFFETT

▼ Knowledge is power

Many people rely on experts to give them advice and this is especially true in the investment world. Friends will often give tips and so will the financial newspapers. Feel free to listen but only if you have the ability to distinguish between what makes sense and what is obviously wrong. I have learned not to risk my money on other people's opinions. You should only invest in stocks that you understand well and are passionate about. The less knowledge you have, the less conviction you should have, and the less reason you have to invest. Focus on that, where you are the expert. Make use of it and it will help you make money.

It is obviously important to do some background research when evaluating a potential trading idea before you spend the time going through all the subsequent steps in the investment process. For instance, if you are interested in a particular retail company, there are things you can do to gain a better understanding of the company, and to help you feel more comfortable about the investment:

1. Visit a few of their stores.
2. Look at the company website and see what information they give to their shareholders.
3. Look for news stories on the Internet.
4. Attend an annual general meeting.
5. Read research by analysts that follow the company. Again the Internet will be of tremendous help with this.
6. Look at a historical chart of the company's stock price.

(You will revisit points 5 and 6 in more detail later on in the investment process, but at this point it can help you identify trading ideas.)

SPECIALIST KNOWLEDGE IS YOUR KEY INVESTMENT EDGE. LEARN TO TRUST YOURSELF.

All this sounds like a lot of work, but this is only because it is something that you are not used to. It is not much harder than choosing a new car; something that most people are reasonably comfortable with, and you will learn quickly enough – as they say, practice makes perfect. Also I am not saying that you should go to an AGM every time you plan to trade, but in the early days it is a good way to gain self-confidence and experience. Don't fall in love with a company: you only want to buy stocks that are going up and sell stocks that have a good chance of going down. Identifying and buying a great company with all the good news already discounted into the stock price is not going to make you money.

If you only focus on one sector, that is fine in the beginning, just make sure you keep your trading size small. Over time you will learn more about other companies and sectors and then you will become more comfortable broadening your portfolio. There is plenty of time to get larger in the future. Remember, even when you are trading within your knowledge comfort zone, you mustn't put all your eggs in one basket. Risk management and good portfolio construction are *always* key to making money long term.

▼ 'Top-down' versus 'bottom-up' investing

Most people take a bottom-up approach to investing. By combining this with the investment framework presented here this is workable, as you are forced to take the world economy and

Bottom-up investing

Looking at individual companies and making investment decisions based on that company's merits.

Top-down investing

Focusing on building a general opinion of the economy and the world and then building a portfolio of stocks that fit within this picture.

> **ALL GREAT TRADERS POSSESS THE COURAGE TO FOLLOW THEIR OWN CONVICTIONS.**

stock market history into account anyway, as well as technical analysis. However, on its own I would consider this a dangerous technique to use; the return on a stock is so dependent on what is going on in the wider market, that just focusing on the stock itself means you often forget that is the case.

You might consider focusing on 'macro' themes as opposed to analysing individual companies as your starting point. This is the way I prefer to trade. Let's say you believe the credit crunch is going to get worse, and perhaps you believe that this will hurt house building companies and banks. You might then look at shorting a few of those names. Or, you may believe we are going to use less air travel going forward, and buy fewer cars – thus airlines and car companies will be affected.

There are so many macro ideas on which to base trades: the world is your oyster. Just choose the ones you feel comfortable with. Make sure that you pick an idea or a theme that has not yet run its course – don't wait for everyone else to have the same idea before you have had the confidence to put on the trade yourself.

▼ Developing your ideas

Once you have had an idea, you then need to process it, and undertake all the fundamental and technical analysis and portfolio checks to make sure you want to put on the trade. This process will be described in the next few sections. Only consider investing when you feel comfortable with your trading idea.

Your idea does not have to be highly original on day one, just get used to the process. If you control your risks well, as I will explain later, you are unlikely to lose much.

Here are a few simple examples to get a flavour. Please don't copy them, as they may no longer be correct, or the market may have priced the news in – and this exercise is all about your ideas and not mine. Once you have put on a few trades you will start to get a feel for the other factors you need to take into account, but for now this is a good start. A later section will include case studies that will describe in much more detail how the idea generation process works in practice.

Idea	Investment	Rationale
Retail sales going up	Buy Next, Marks & Spencer	Good for retailers
I think the oil price is going up	Sell British Airways, Buy BP	Good for oil producers, bad for airlines
Copper is going up	Buy Xtrata, BHP Billiton	Mining benefits
House prices are going down	Sell Wolseley, British Land	Building material suppliers and property developers suffer
Taxes are going up on cigarettes and alcohol	Sell BAT, Punch Taverns	Not good for either
Sterling is crashing	Buy Diageo, AstraZeneca	Large exporters have higher profits when translated back into Sterling
I am worried about the economy	Buy Tesco, Unilever, National Grid	Defensive names are relatively safe
I believe the China story	Buy HSBC	Large China exposure

Names to know: Peter Lynch

Peter Lynch (1944–) is widely accepted as one of the world's best fund managers. He started as a research analyst at Fidelity Investments in 1966. In 1977 he was given responsibility for managing a small fund called the Magellan Fund. The fund had $18 million when he started, and $14 billion when he retired in 1990, making on average 29% per year. This made it the top-performing fund in the world in its sector. In a similar way to Warren Buffett, Lynch believed strongly in only investing in what you know, and selected undervalued stocks based on bottom-up, fundamental analysis. He paid little attention to market direction or timing.

Peter Lynch believed in using 'local knowledge' and common sense to produce fantastic investment ideas. Many of his own originated when he was out with his family as opposed to reading research reports. He believed that everyone could be involved in first-hand analysis by observing his or her own consumer purchases. His analysis of stocks however did not end there – diligent research was a cornerstone of his investment approach.

Lynch considered it futile to predict the economy and interest rates. He is well known for saying 'If you spend more than 13 minutes analyzing economic and market forecasts you've wasted ten minutes.'

He was always on the search for that stock that would go up ten-fold, the 'ten bagger' as he called it, and held on to it once he thought he found it. In his famous book *One Up on Wall Street*, Lynch suggests only buying a stock for reasons that you could easily explain to an eight-year-old. He had a reputation for working around the clock, and for being in constant contact with a multitude of company managers, brokers and analysts.

►Part 4

Analysing companies

The man who is generally regarded as the greatest investor of our time, Warren Buffett (who also happens to be the richest man on earth), is a fundamental investor. He did not inherit his wealth or plunder his country, he made it all himself. Buffett does not worry too much about the stock market on a day-to-day basis. He just wants to own great companies run by excellent management teams. He does not want to pay over the odds for these businesses and wants to understand exactly where and how they make their money – unfortunately this is not as easy as it sounds.

Analysing companies, sometimes called fundamental analysis, uses historical and present data to make financial forecasts about the future earnings of a company. The ultimate goal is to conduct a company stock valuation and predict the future stock price.

COMMON MISCONCEPTION: A good stock is the same as a good company

Some companies are amazing: they make a great product, management is skilful and experienced, and the brand is really cool. However, the stock might not have moved up for years and neither will it do so in the future.

For our purposes, a good stock is a stock that goes up when we buy it, and down after we sell it, i.e. a stock that makes you money. This can be any stock; it doesn't matter which one you choose, as long as it makes money. These are the stocks that we should be looking for – never fall in love with a company because it will cloud your judgement and could end up costing you money.

▼ The analyst's view: limitations

In my 19 years of trading I have never seen real benefits from looking at fundamental analysis in isolation. This may sound odd, but let me tell you why. Most big companies are researched by many different analysts. These analysts look at all the financial statements, visit the company several times a year, and know the relevant industry inside out. After all this hard work, the analysts make their recommendations, and set price targets for the stocks that they follow. And here is the amazing thing: there is a huge margin of variation in their recommendations.

For example, here are the last six recommendations on Nokia. (At the time of writing, the Nokia stock price was 12.50 Euros.)

Firm	Recommendation	Target price (Euros)
Broker 1	Sell/Cautious	9.4
Broker 2	Buy	16
Broker 3	Add	15
Broker 4	Buy	21
Broker 5	Sell	11.5
Broker 6	Neutral	16

There is clearly a huge difference in the analysts' opinions on this stock. One analyst thinks I can make 68% by buying the stock (from 12.50 to 21 Euros), while another one thinks I can make 25% by selling it (from 12.5 to 9.4)!

So which analyst am I going to believe? I have no idea. Sometimes there are rankings available, but my experience is that there is no correlation between the ranking of a research analyst, and his future predictions being correct. Obviously, by the time you read this book, the ratings and price targets will have long changed.

Target price

Target price: an analyst's estimate of the price of a stock at some point in the future.

These differences in opinion also exist for other stocks – often to a greater degree. The variations seen in these target prices and recommendations are a result of a combination of several different factors:

1. Differences in assumptions

Calculating a target price for a big company is very complicated and is based on many different assumptions. To calculate the profits of Nokia it is very important to make an assumption about worldwide sales of handsets. Different analysts will have different opinions on this number and this will lead to different target prices. They also need to develop a view on which particular handset will sell more, the cheaper ones or the more expensive ones, each with their own profit margin. They need to estimate the tax rate of the company and the interest rate at which it can borrow money. They will need to estimate how aggressive the competitors will be and how funky the designs are of models that have not yet been thought about. I can think of many more variables that an analyst should take into account but I think you get my point. In my opinion it is mission impossible, and also very dependent on the economic situation.

After the analysts have made their own assumptions about the future earnings of a company, they then have to try and guess what others are willing to pay for those expected earnings, and call it a 'valuation'. As an individual, I have little opportunity to add value if I conduct this analysis myself, and it is unlikely that my forecast will be better than the average forecast of all the different analysts.

2. Conflicts of interest

Another fact of life is that many analysts have conflicts of interest. The companies they follow may be current or future clients of the bank they work for. A company may seek advice if it is planning to take over another company or if it is taken over itself, and if the research analyst from a particular bank has been negative about the management of that business, the company is not likely to ask for that bank's advice – and the analyst could miss out on a big

Names to know: Warren Buffett

Warren Buffett (1930–) from Omaha, Nebraska, is the most successful investor in history. He started with nothing, but is currently the richest man in the world, with a fortune of close to $60 billion. He is the CEO and Chairman of Berkshire Hathaway, a company that he bought in the early 1960s when it was a distressed textile company, and which now combines all his business interests. These interests centre around insurance and reinsurance, but also on world famous brands such as Coca-Cola, American Express, Goldman Sachs, Harley Davidson and Gillette.

Buffett's investment style has been heavily influenced by Benjamin Graham – the father of value investing. In fact, Buffett sought him out and studied under him at Columbia Business School, and eventually worked with him at his partnership. Simply put, Buffett invests in undervalued companies that he considers to be well run, and which he expects will grow indefinitely.

Buffett does not like investing in companies with a lot of debt: 'Good business or investment decisions will eventually produce quite satisfactory economic results, with no aid from leverage.' Buffett also believes that the company business should be easily understood. He was criticised for not investing in technology stocks during the dot.com bubble but Buffett, a self-proclaimed technophobe, refused to invest in companies that did not meet his criteria. Ultimately his devotion to his own rules saved him when the Internet bubble burst.

Every year thousand of shareholders come to the AGM of Berkshire Hathaway to listen to the 'Sage of Omaha'. It is the most widely known Chairman's speech in the whole financial world. He has also made the highest ever donation to charity: in 2006 he donated over $25 billion to the Bill and Melinda Gates Foundation.

bonus. Companies usually choose banks where the analyst has been positive about their performance. Financial regulators have been addressing this issue, and rightly so, but only with mixed success.

3. Belief in company management
Another problem is that analysts tend to over-rely on what company management tells them.

You would hope that management is prudent, but in reality they are often too optimistic, and have trouble seeing the wood from the trees. Research shows that they suffer from as much over-confidence and over-optimism as the rest of us. And they may not be telling us the whole story; in the worst cases management is outright fraudulent. It is hard for an analyst to take into account in his analysis that management might be lying, but you should!

4. Hearts can sometimes rule heads
Analysts have a tendency to fall in love with a stock independent of what the stock price is doing as they get to know company

▶ ▶ The inside track   **Enron**

The case of Enron, a huge energy trading company in the US, is a prime example. Rumours had been circulating for a while that the company might be in trouble. However, at some point in 2001, the Goldman Sachs analyst spoke to management and afterwards told investors he felt very comfortable with the company. He produced a research report and reiterated his 'recommended list' rating. Within a few days the company filed for bankruptcy and the stock was worthless. This was a case of serious fraud: the directors went to jail and one of them committed suicide. Company management do not tell analysts when they are committing fraud, thus rendering the fundamental data incorrect, and the whole analysis redundant.

> **COMMON MISCONCEPTION:** Company
> management has the same goals as its shareholders

In theory, the owners of a company, i.e. the shareholders, appoint a management team to run the company on a day-to-day basis.

In practice there can be tens of thousands of different shareholders and company management tends to use its discretion when running the company, as they cannot possibly consult all these shareholders every time a decision needs to be made. This can cause friction between shareholders and company management, especially when management is of the opinion that shareholders do not really understand their business.

What is also becoming increasingly apparent is that too often management pay has little to do with competence but everything to do with the contracts they have negotiated. There is a view that if they spent as much time and diligence negotiating the contracts that impact the future of the company they work for, as they do with their own employment contracts, we would not be in the economic mess as we are today.

A cynic would say that management is interested in pushing the stock price as high as possible, so that they can cash in their stock options. Management would probably reply that this high stock price is in the interest of all shareholders. True in theory, but not in practice, because most shareholders hold on to their stock for the long term, by which time company management has often moved on, and the stock price is not looking so good. It seems fair that management is rewarded for long-term success, but to be compensated for failure, as so often has been the case, seems extremely unfair to shareholders, and other stakeholders such as employees.

management over the years. This in itself is no problem; however they often become too close to remain totally objective. It takes a strong person to put out a sell recommendation if they are best friends with the CEO. When the stock is a buy at 10, a buy when it goes to 30, but still a buy when it has dropped to 5, the analysis has become useless.

▼ Company performance: basic concepts

Having said all this, it is still important to be aware of a few fundamental concepts as they will help you compare individual companies, their sector, and the market overall. They can also show you how the company valuation has changed over time.

Let's begin by looking at a balance sheet and an income statement, as they are the source of a lot of fundamental analysis. This might look complicated at first, but it is just a question of getting used to it, and it is a way of thinking that might help you when managing your own finances. You can find the necessary information on the Internet and on the company website.

▷ The balance sheet

This table represents a single point in time, usually at financial year-end, and can therefore be manipulated in order to present the company in the best possible light. The left side shows assets owned by the company, such as tools, a factory, cash in the bank etc., and the right side shows who the company owes money to, and what is left over, and thus owned by the shareholders.

Assets	Liabilities and Owners' Equity
Cash £100 million	Notes Payable £20 million
Accounts Receivable £50 million	Accounts Payable £40 million
Total: Current Assets £150 million	Total: Total Liabilities £60 million
	Capital Stock £50 million
Tools and Equipment £30 million	Retained Earnings £70 million
Total: Fixed Assets £30 million	Total: Owners' Equity £120 million
Total Assets: £180 million	Total: £180 million

▷ The income statement

This includes all the sales made by the company and deducts all the expenses relating to these sales and running the company. The bottom line is called net income.

Sales	£500 million
Cost of goods sold	£300 million
Gross profit	£200 million
Salaries	£40 million
Advertising	£10 million
Rent	£20 million
Utilities	£10 million
Depreciation	£20 million
Net income before taxes	£100 million
Taxes	£30 million
Net Income (Earnings)	£70 million

▷ Financial ratios

There are four main financial ratios you need to know about:

1. The liquidity ratio

Personally, I would rather invest in a company that has plenty of cash and little debt, than a company that has taken on so much

Liquidity ratio

Short-term assets divided by short-term liabilities.

debt that any slight setback could make the company insolvent. That's where the liquidity ratio comes in.

The liquidity ratio compares the cash in the company's bank account to its short-term debt. A ratio greater than two is considered relatively safe, and means that the cash (and cash equivalents) that the company has in the bank, is sufficient to pay its debts for the next two years. The lower the ratio, the more a company is dependent on the bank, and the higher the chance of a company defaulting during periods such as the recent credit crunch.

2. The debt ratio
This is the same as the liquidity ratio, but looks at a company's ability to pay long-term debt. If you have a lot of debt outstanding, it means you have less to fall back on when interest rates go up.

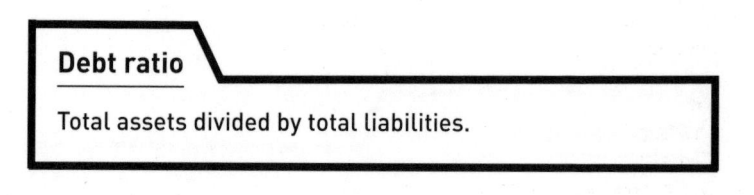

Debt ratio

Total assets divided by total liabilities.

3. The profitability ratio
Before investing in a company, I want to know how profitable that company is, as I want to see if it is generating an acceptable rate of return.

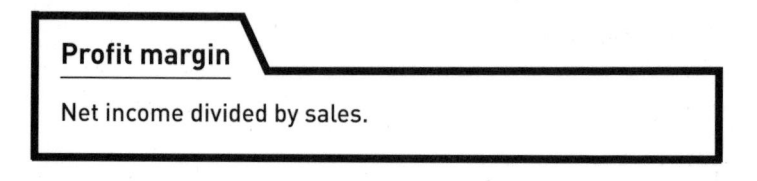

Profit margin

Net income divided by sales.

If a company makes 20p profit for every £1 they sell it is preferable to making only 5p. Having said that the nature of a business can mean that some companies, e.g. food retailers, are subject to structurally low returns so you have to look at this ratio on a case-by-case basis. Return on capital is net income divided by invested capital. Obviously an investor wants the company to make more money in the course of its business than he would get by just putting his money in a 'risk-free' bank account.

4. Market ratios

These tend to be the most relevant ratios from a trader's perspective. They compare fundamental company data to actual market prices.

There are three main ratios to discuss here.

a. Price to earnings (P/E) ratio

This shows how many years' earnings the stock is trading at in the stock market; the higher the P/E, the more expensive the company.

Price to earnings ratio

Stock price divided by earnings per share.

Better-run companies tend to have higher P/Es, and so do fast-growing companies, because the market believes the right earnings to look at are not this year's earnings, but future earnings. Remember that we have already learned that buying stock with high P/Es is often wrong (see p.66).

You should always look at next year's earnings as well ('forward earnings'). P/Es are useful, but be careful before deciding to invest based on this ratio in isolation.

b. Price to book (P/B) ratio

The book value is that part of the company owned by shareholders, i.e. assets minus liabilities. Looking back at the balance sheet, it is the capital stock plus the retained earnings. The ratio shows how many times the book value investors are prepared to pay for the company.

Price to book ratio

Stock price divided by book value per share.

In case of bankruptcy the company's value is close to its book value. If investors are worried about the business the stock will trade close to a P/B of 1. If people do not trust the balance sheet and data the company management provides, then the P/B ratio can easily go below one.

c. EV/EBITDA

As P/E's are quite difficult to compare across industries, another ratio, EV to EBITDA, has grown in importance over the last few years. Similar to the P/E, it shows how much investors are prepared to pay in terms of the company's earnings.

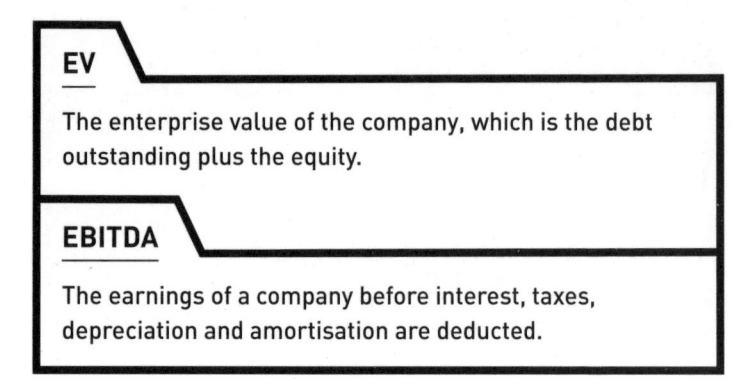

EV

The enterprise value of the company, which is the debt outstanding plus the equity.

EBITDA

The earnings of a company before interest, taxes, depreciation and amortisation are deducted.

Names to know: Benjamin Graham

Benjamin Graham (1894–1976) is the author of the two main books on fundamental investing, *Security Analysis* (1934) and *The Intelligent Investor* (1949).

He was born in London, and moved to Brooklyn, New York, as a baby. The world's richest man and most respected investor, Warren Buffett, cites Graham, his former lecturer at Columbia University, as his investment guru. Benjamin Graham's main focus was value investing. He was only interested in buying stocks that were very cheap.

In an interview he gave in 1976, Graham was asked to give some rules for individual investors. Two of these were:

1. 'The individual investor should act consistently as an investor and not as a speculator. This means, in sum, that he should be able to justify every purchase he makes and each price he pays by impersonal, objective reasoning that satisfies him that he is getting more than his money's worth for his purchase – in other words, that he has a margin of safety, in value terms, to protect his commitment.'

2. 'The investor should have a definite selling policy for all his common stock commitments, corresponding to his buying techniques. Typically, he should set a reasonable profit objective on each purchase – say 50 to 100% – and a maximum holding period for this objective to be realized – say, two to three years. Purchases not realizing the gain objective at the end of the holding period should be sold out at the market.'

In the same interview he said, 'It is fortunate for Wall Street as an institution that a small minority of people can trade successfully and that many others think they can'.

▷ The margin of safety

Warren Buffet always cites Benjamin Graham as his greatest influence as far as investing is concerned. Graham's book, *Security Analysis*, which was published in 1934, is regarded as the bible of fundamental analysis. One key concept from the book is called the 'margin of safety'.

Margin of safety

The difference between the intrinsic value of a stock and its market price or also as the price at which a share investment can be bought with minimal downside risk.

A common interpretation of the margin of safety is how far below its intrinsic value one is paying for a stock. For high quality issues, value investors typically want to pay 90 cents on the dollar (90% of intrinsic value) while more speculative stocks should be purchased for up to a 50% discount to intrinsic value (pay 50 cents on the dollar). Intrinsic value is quite a difficult concept to grasp, and is based on how much it would cost to recreate an (economically viable) company in the most efficient manner.

▼ It's all about the numbers

The majority of people will not look at a balance sheet or income statement before investing. I am not telling you that you should, but you need to be aware that a company has obligations to pay the interest on its debt, before it can pay you a dividend. So to avoid investing in the dark you need to find out how large that debt really is. You also need to understand when you are paying a high P/E multiple and thus have less chance of making money. Please realise that you cannot always believe what you are being told, either by a company analyst or by management.

It is clear that analysing companies is all about making the right assumptions and looking at the right numbers. To do this you need to think about the company's customers, the industry itself, and what will happen to them in the near and the more distant future. You might have a great company in a great sector but if their main product is going to be replaced by a cheaper, more efficient alternative in a few years, you might not want to be a shareholder. Many companies will go the same way as the economy. It is risky buying a cyclical stock just as the business cycle goes south, and the chances are that the earnings will have to be downgraded.

The stock chart analysis discussed in the next section complements this analysis as the charts can be seen as the aggregate conclusion of all market participants about a certain stock.

> 'GO FOR A BUSINESS THAT ANY IDIOT CAN RUN – BECAUSE SOONER OR LATER, ANY IDIOT IS PROBABLY GOING TO RUN IT.'
>
> PETER LYNCH

►Part 5

Analysing stock movements

Technical analysis aims to forecast future stock prices by analysing past stock movements. This is done using stock charts that show the past price levels of a stock, i.e. what people have been willing to pay for that stock over time.

Using historical charts to tell you where the stock will trade in the future probably sounds like a dark art to the novice, and in some ways it is. However, many professional investors look at charts, perhaps not to help them make an actual trading decision, but to help them judge the timing of a purchase or sale. Technical analysts believe that markets are efficient, i.e. that the combined knowledge of all market participants is priced in, and that it doesn't matter what business a company is in. In fact, they don't really care about companies themselves, they just care about stocks; good stocks are those that make them money, whether their prices are going up or down.

▼ Trending or ranging?

When I look at a chart I try to form an opinion on whether the stock is trending or ranging.

If the stock trends there is a clear direction up or down, if it ranges it stays within defined bands. Obviously you don't really want to buy a stock for the longer term if it is only ranging – you need to find a stock that will trend higher.

The top of a range tends to be the level at which there could be some large sellers of the stock. Other market participants might be aware of this and add to the selling pressure at this level. That level is called technical resistance.

The bottom of the range might be a level where deep value investors believe it is a good investment to buy some stock for the

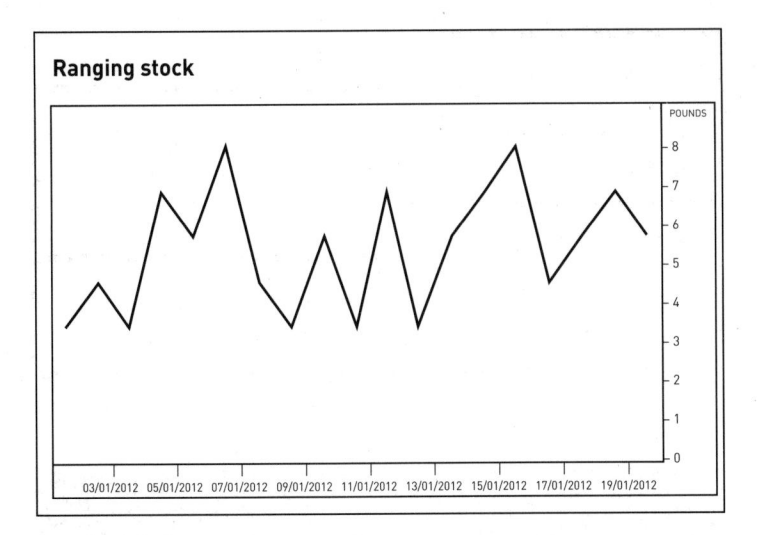

Ranging stock

POUNDS

8
7
6
5
4
3
2
1
0

03/01/2012 05/01/2012 07/01/2012 09/01/2012 11/01/2012 13/01/2012 15/01/2012 17/01/2012 19/01/2012

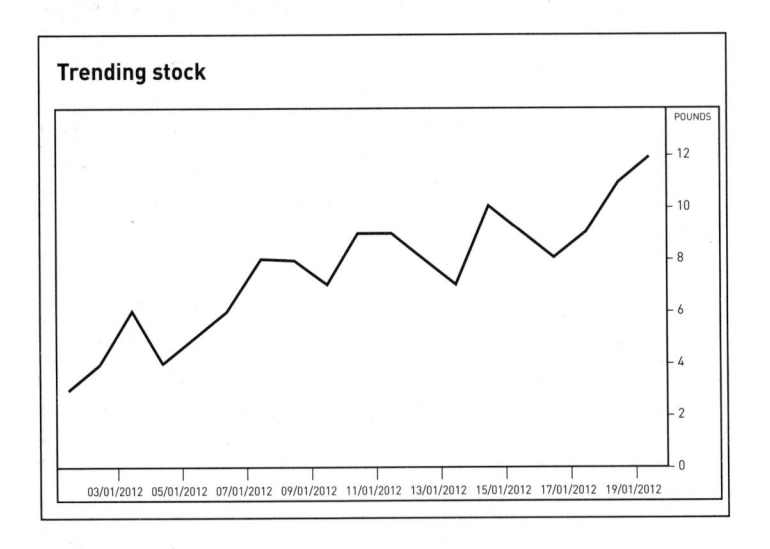

Trending stock

POUNDS

12
10
8
6
4
2
0

03/01/2012 05/01/2012 07/01/2012 09/01/2012 11/01/2012 13/01/2012 15/01/2012 17/01/2012 19/01/2012

long term; the stock will not go below this price as long as these people still have buying power. This price level might represent a short-term bottom in the stock chart and is called technical support. A range has a level of support at one fixed price level. An uptrend has support at an ever-rising level. If this support level is breached the uptrend could be over.

Technical resistance

A level where prices find it hard to trade above. This is normally because of the presence of large sellers.

Technical support

The level at which a stock does not trade below. This is often because of a large buying interest.

▶ ▶ The inside track
Trending and ranging

If I am looking to buy a stock the first thing I do is to look at a chart and identify where the stock is trading. A stock might be a great buy for fundamental reasons but if I see that it is already trading at the top of its range I usually prefer to wait. It is possible that the reasons why I wanted to buy it have already been priced in and I have missed it for the moment.

So, if I decide to buy this stock I will have to wait until the stock goes back down to the lower part of the range. If a stock is trending up, it is slightly less important where I buy as I need to ensure that I do not miss the trend, but the principle of aiming to buy at the lower end of the range is still valid.

The same is true when I want to sell or short sell a stock. If the stock is already trading at the low I must assume I have missed it. This is obviously not always true, and a new low can be a great sell signal, but for purposes of this book it is the safest way to trade. Timing is everything in trading. It is a very expensive luxury not to take the charts into account when you buy or sell a stock.

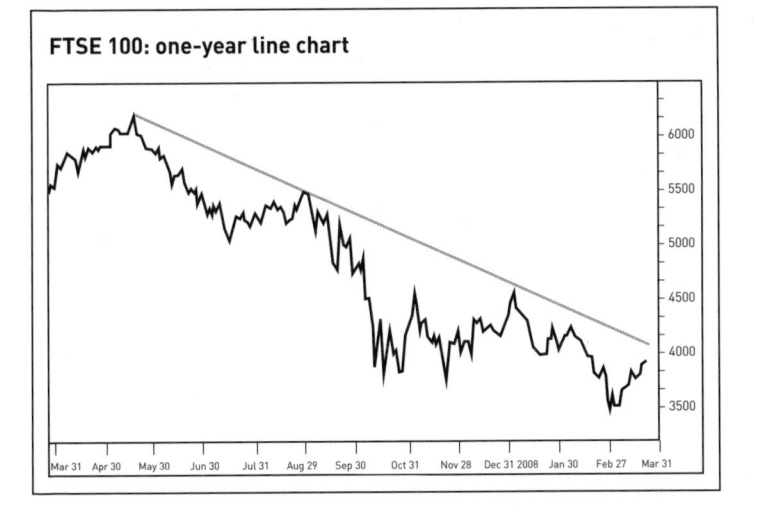

FTSE 100: one-year line chart

Y-axis values: 6000, 5500, 5000, 4500, 4000, 3500

X-axis labels: Mar 31, Apr 30, May 30, Jun 30, Jul 31, Aug 29, Sep 30, Oct 31, Nov 28, Dec 31 2008, Jan 30, Feb 27, Mar 31

On this chart I have drawn a trend line that shows the downtrend in the FTSE for the year ending March 2009. In order for me to become more bullish, I needed to see the FTSE break this downtrend (which it did). It is quite an obvious line, and if the stock starts trading above this downward sloping line ('break out'), this will attract new buyers and make people who are short the market less certain of their positions. The reason that it attracts new buyers is that a lot of people trade based on technicals and the break of a clearly defined trend line does not go unnoticed.

Break out

The overcoming of technical resistance. The buyers are more powerful than the sellers who have now run out of ammunition.

TIMING IS EVERYTHING IN TRADING.

▼ Building up the technical picture

The whole idea of looking at a chart is to try and establish if the current price is an attractive price at which to buy or sell a certain stock.

When forming a technical picture, and trying to predict the likely direction of a chart in the future, there are several more things to consider.

▷ Time periods

When I am trying to establish if a stock is ranging or trending I don't just look at one time period; I look at several periods, sometimes as many as five, before I can draw a meaningful conclusion.

Looking at these different time periods helps me get a sense of the major and minor trends for the stock/index, and puts them into context; you don't want to be buying something that looked good for five days, but the last three months and three years looked awful, unless you have a very good reason.

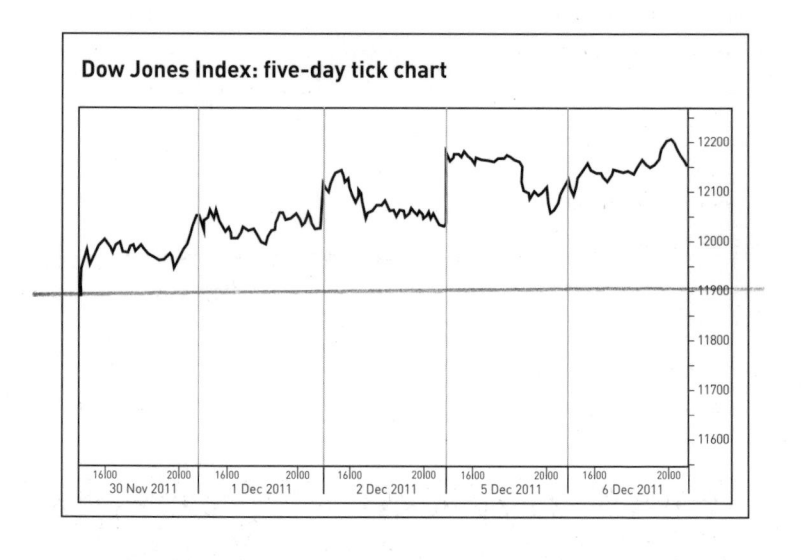

Dow Jones Index: five-day tick chart

Let's take the Dow Jones Index as an example. The Dow Jones comprises the 30 largest stocks in the US. We can analyse this index over different time periods. Let's look at a tick chart, a one-year chart, a five-year chart, a 20-year chart and a 60-year chart. That will give us a pretty good idea of where we are in stock market history.

The chart (previous page) shows that the Dow had had a good five days with a continuous uptrend of about 300 points, i.e. more than 2%. Not a bad week.

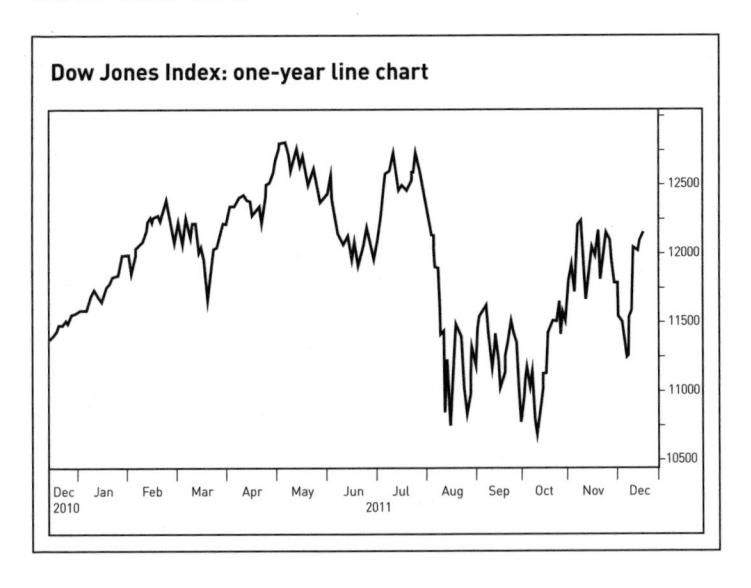

Dow Jones Index: one-year line chart

The one-year trend looks very different; the market has been all over the place but 'happens' to be 5% above the level of a year ago which shows again that a 2% return in a week is really good.

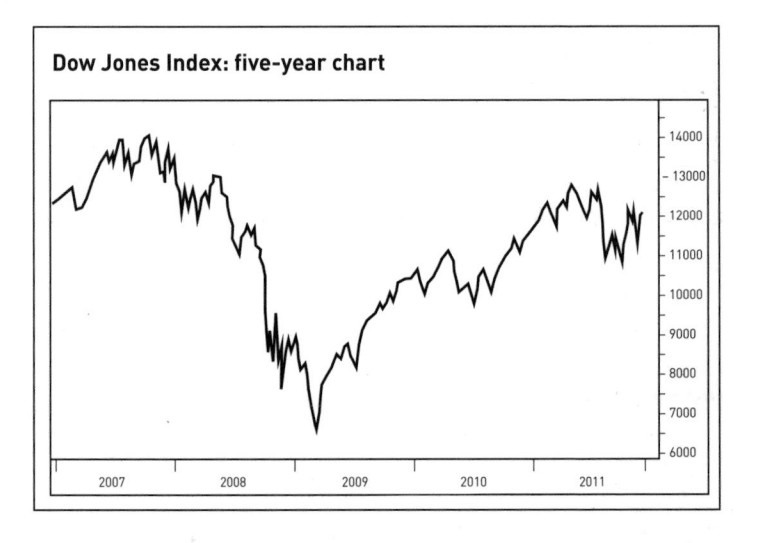

Dow Jones Index: five-year chart

The chart above shows five years of data. The Dow is now only just back at the level where it was five years ago! That is a long period without capital appreciation.

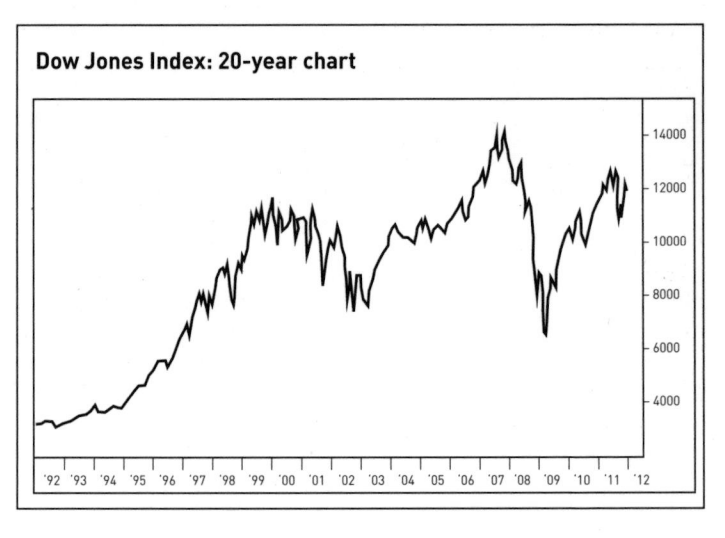

Dow Jones Index: 20-year chart

The 20-year chart shows that if you had bought stocks around 1992 you would have done very well, but any time since 2000 has clearly not been great. Equities might be for the long term – if (and this is a big 'if') you are able to time it perfectly.

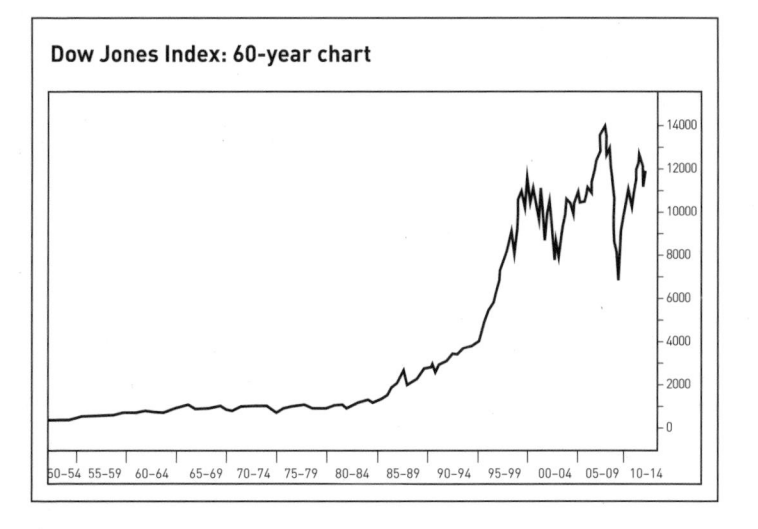

Dow Jones Index: 60-year chart

The above chart shows equities may be a good investment if your time horizon is long enough; hopefully you know better by now. And this chart does not look bullish to me either ...

All this goes to show that you need to look at a range of charts to determine exactly where you are in history. If you are used to the Dow trading between 12,000 and 14,000 it is quite hard to imagine it trading much below those levels. However, if you go back in history, you will see that trading below these levels is the norm rather than the exception.

▷ Open/high/low/close charts

The charts shown so far have been normal line charts. The charts I tend to use myself are open/high/low/close charts. These show the high, the low, the opening price and the closing price for each day of trading.

Every stripe on the chart below has a little dash to the left and one to the right. The one on the left is the opening price, the one to the right is the closing price. The highest level on the stripe is the high of the day, and the lowest level is the low on that day. This gives you a lot more information than the usual line chart, which

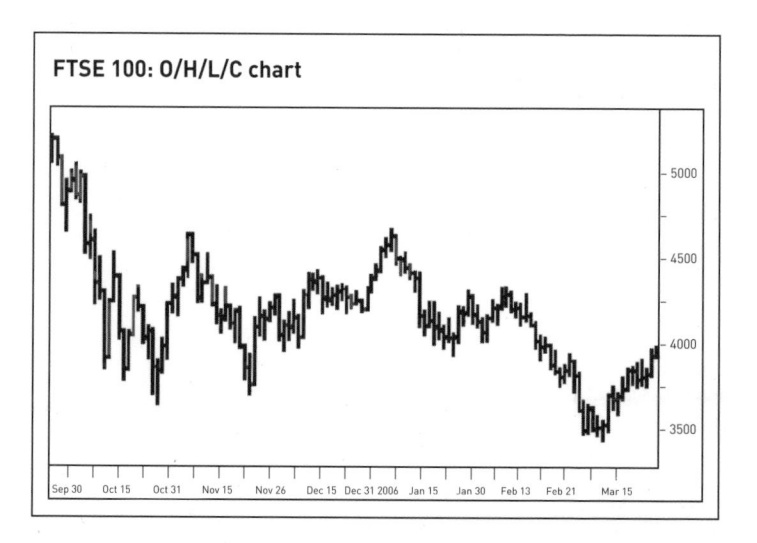

FTSE 100: O/H/L/C chart

shows the closing price of the day, but gives no information on what happened during the day. For example, if a stock opens at the low but closes at the high it is more bullish than the other way around. This can be valuable information.

▷ Volume

An important technical indicator to look at is the volume, or the amount of shares that trade on any given day. When a price moves on high volume, that new price is more significant than when the price of the stock moves on a quiet day. Volume is printed at the bottom of the graph (as per chart on p.109).

Volume

The amount of shares that trade on any given day.

▷ Moving averages

Sometimes people look at a moving average to smooth out price action in order to eliminate short-term price movements that could cloud the overall trend. A moving average is the average

> ### Moving Average
>
> The average price over a certain number of days. If the
> last five prices were 8, 10, 12, 15, 15, the five day
> moving average will be 12 and the three day moving
> average will be 14.

price a stock has traded at over a given number of days. A short
term moving average could be five days, while a long-term moving
average could be as much as a year.

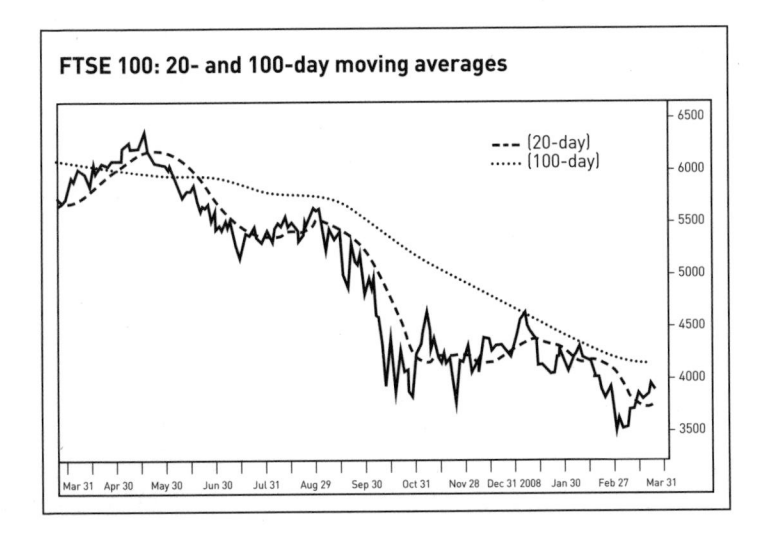

FTSE 100: 20- and 100-day moving averages

A potentially good buy signal is given when a shorter-term moving
average crosses from below to above a longer-term moving
average. For example, if a stock has traded down over the last
year or so, it might make sense to wait before buying it until the
20-day moving average trades above the 100-day moving average,
as in the chart above. By the way, shorting the FTSE when the 20-
day broke the 100-day from above to below, would have kept you
short for pretty much the whole down move, potentially making
you a good return.

▷ The Relative Strength Index

Before I buy or sell a stock I want to see if my idea is original or a bit too obvious. I need to know if am going with the 'consensus' view, or if I am contrarian, and going against the consensus. If lots of other people have bought the same stock recently, the chances are that the stock has gone up too much too quickly, and in this case the stock is known as 'overbought'. If a stock has sold off too much too fast it is called 'oversold'.

The one indicator I use for this is the Relative Strength Index (RSI). The RSI index is a formula that tries to capture what has happened to a stock in the short term. A low number means it has sold off recently, while a high number means that a lot of buyers have been active in the stock. The RSI varies between 0 and 100. Above 70 is considered overbought, below 30 is oversold. When you are looking to take a new position, but the RSI is below 30 and doom and gloom is on the front page of the *Financial Times*, it might well mean that you are too late to short sell for now and should wait for a bounce.

The chart below shows the RSI for mining company BHP Billiton. It is normally drawn below the price chart. The stock is starting to look overbought short term. Be aware though, if a stock has been ranging for a while and is at the top of the range, the stock will look overbought. However, if it breaks out after ranging for this long the break out could be really important, as the sellers are no longer present at that level. So if the RSI deters you from buying you might miss a massive break out.

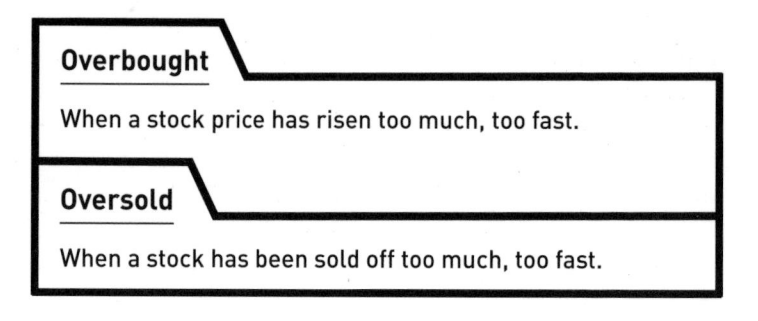

Overbought

When a stock price has risen too much, too fast.

Oversold

When a stock has been sold off too much, too fast.

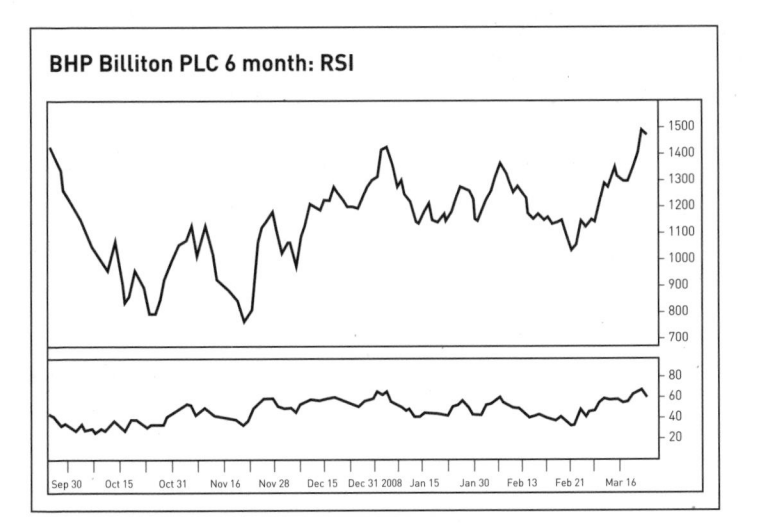

BHP Billiton PLC 6 month: RSI

▼ Classic stock patterns

Once we have an idea whether a stock has been trending or ranging over its history we need to work out if this will continue into the future. To achieve this we need to find either a continuation or a reversal pattern in the chart.

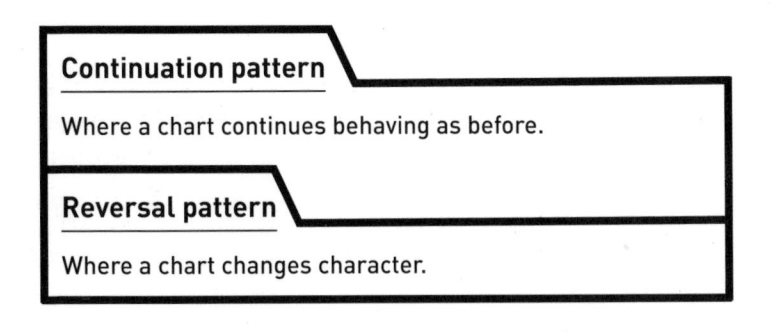

Continuation pattern

Where a chart continues behaving as before.

Reversal pattern

Where a chart changes character.

▷ Reversal patterns

First we will look at two reversal patterns.

1. The first reversal pattern is a head and shoulder pattern.

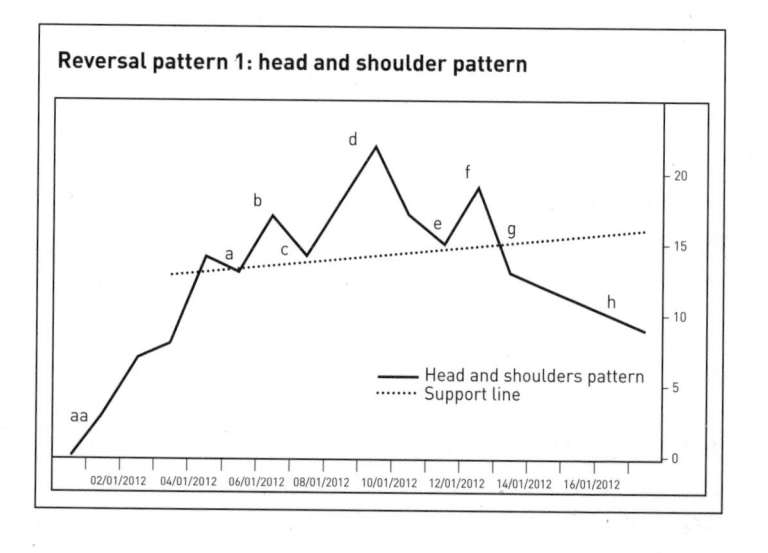

Reversal pattern 1: head and shoulder pattern

The area between a and c is known as the 'left shoulder', the area between c and e is the 'head', and between e and g is the 'right shoulder'.

This stock was trending up from point aa with no real setbacks until it reached point b. It then traded down (sold off) until it reached point c, before continuing the rally to point d. The uptrend was still persisting. However, when it sold off to point e it started to look as if the uptrend was broken. There was one last attempt to rally, but when it did not make a new high at f, it looked as if the price at d was going to remain as the high. When the chart broke support at g, the head and shoulder pattern was complete.

The most likely outcome is that prices will now remain below the previous support line (called the 'neck line' in the case of a head and shoulders pattern), and that the stock is no longer trending up. In fact the trend has reversed and the next price target for the stock is somewhere in the 'belly' region.

The volume, or the amount of shares that trade on any given day, is also important. In this head and shoulders, if the volume between e and f is lower than the volume between f and g, this shows that the buyers are running out of power and makes it more likely to be a genuine head and shoulders pattern, which if this is the case, makes it a more reliable sell signal.

While a normal head and shoulders is a bearish pattern, you can also imagine a reverse graph, which is known as a reverse head and shoulders – this is a bullish pattern.

2. A double top pattern
Resembling an 'M' shape, this is a pattern where a stock hits resistance (at a), trades down (sells off), and then has another failed attempt to break through the resistance level (at b) before falling again.

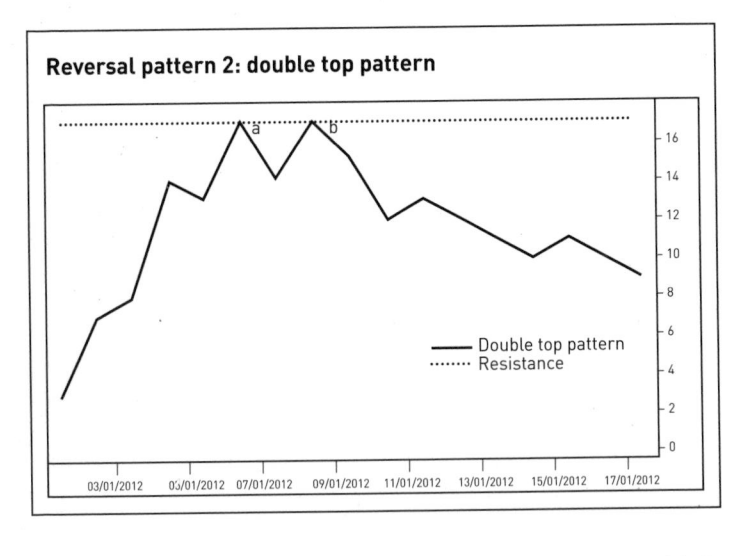

Sometimes the stock will try to break through a third time; this is called a triple top. The more times a stock price bounces off a resistance level, the more important the technical pattern. The less volume trades at the next attempt to break this level, the more significant the pattern. This is another trend reversal pattern.

An opposite pattern is also possible, where a stock has been falling, but now hits a double bottom. That pattern suggests the bearish trend has been broken and the stock might now start ranging or even trending up.

▷ Continuation patterns

Flags and pennants are two examples of continuation patterns.

A bullish flag occurs after a rally in the stock price, when the stock pauses and starts forming a slightly downward sloping range, within well-defined boundaries. Normally volumes drop before the stock makes its final move, breaks out of the range to the upside, and continues the uptrend.

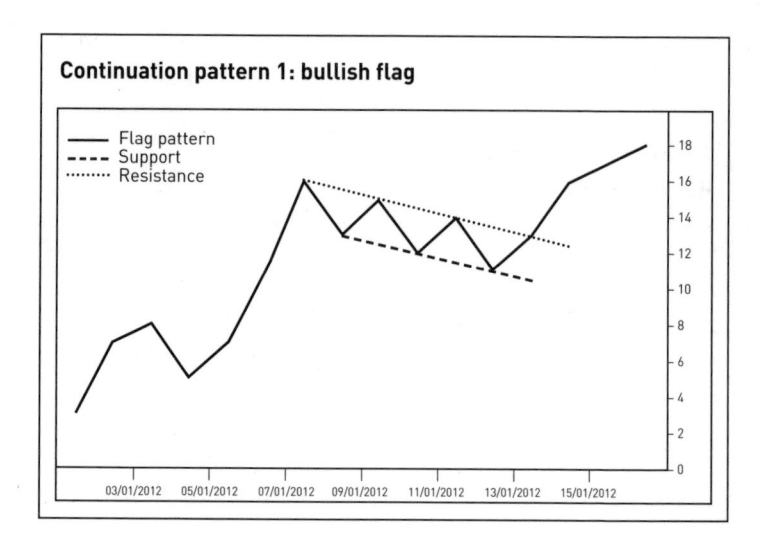

A bullish pennant looks like a flag as well, has similar theory behind it and appears as below. A pennant differs from a flag in that the prices are not ranging but form a triangle pattern. Inverting these charts will show their bearish equivalents.

If you want to find out more, read *Technical Analysis of the Financial Markets* by John J. Murphy – the 'bible' of this subject.

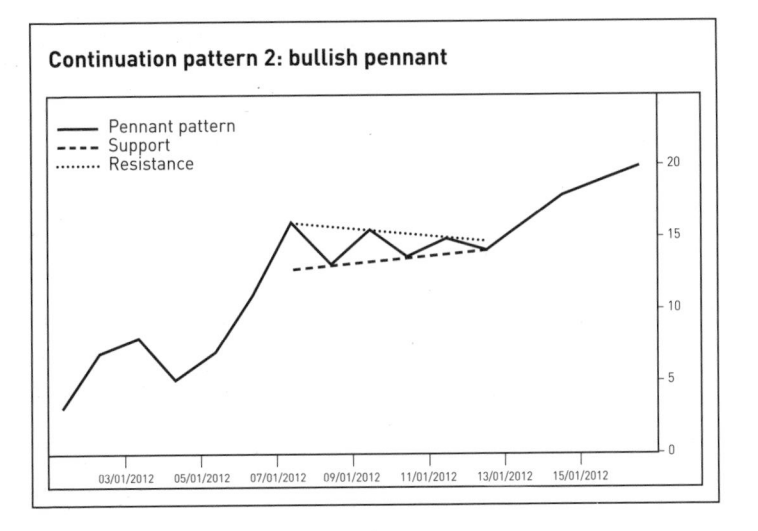

Continuation pattern 2: bullish pennant

— Pennant pattern
- - - Support
.... Resistance

▼ Spotting trading opportunities

To spot trading opportunities you need to identify those trades that have the odds in your favour. You can do this by combining the stock chart with one or more of the indicators we have already looked at, such as volume, moving averages or the Relative Strength Index.

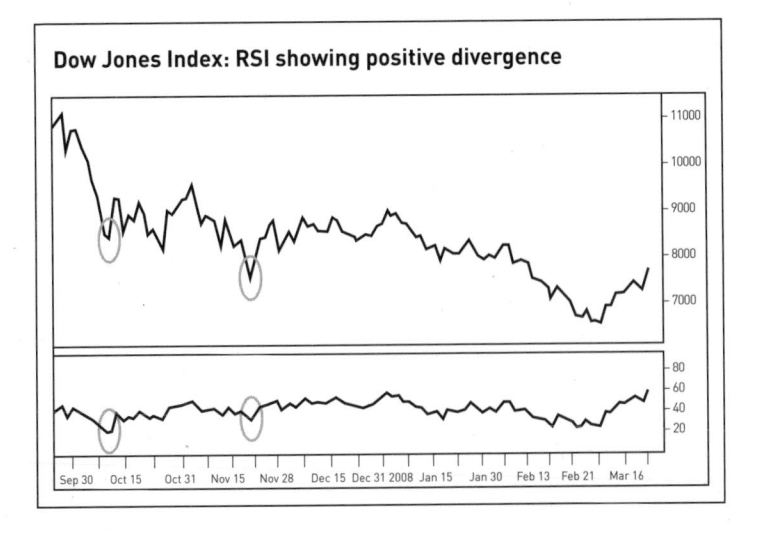

Dow Jones Index: RSI showing positive divergence

For example, let's look at a Dow chart. When the Dow in the price chart above made a new low, it was not confirmed by a new low on the RSI. This phenomenon is called positive divergence. The market made a new low but the RSI did not. This divergence from the RSI gave a buy signal.

Or look at the chart below which shows that the gold Exchange Traded Fund (ETF) has recently been trading less volume on days that the price was down, than on days that the price went up. Even though prices have been going lower which is a negative this has not been because a large number of people were selling, which is a positive. So when the stock starts going up again and it is accompanied by high shares volume it might make you now want to buy this stock; something that you would not have identified by looking at a line chart alone. Using extra technical tools when analysing a stock chart will give you a higher chance of being correct and thus making money.

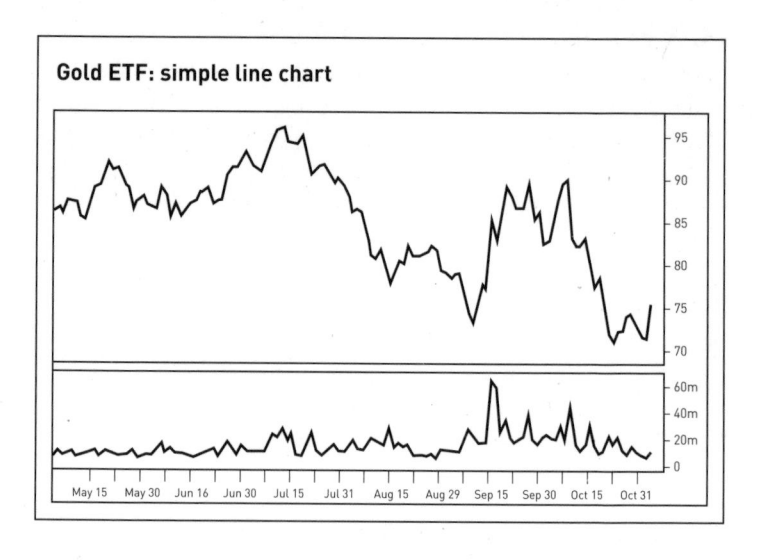

Gold ETF: simple line chart

As an example of 'pattern recognition' we can take the example of crude oil in October 2008, as seen in the chart below, where a bearish flag formation appeared.

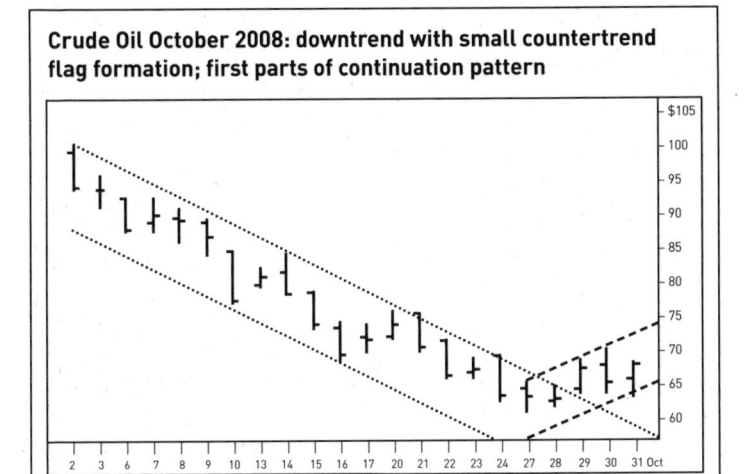

Crude Oil October 2008: downtrend with small countertrend flag formation; first parts of continuation pattern

This is a continuation pattern, and was a text book example, followed by a further sell-off over the next three weeks.

▼ Sourcing the information

You might wonder where you can get these stock charts if you are not a professional investor. It is actually quite straightforward: if you have a trading account your broker should provide them free of charge. If you don't, all you need to do is search the Internet using 'chart', followed by the stock name, and it will refer you to many different websites that will provide it for you.

I love looking at charts. They give me a good idea of what has happened to a stock price over the past weeks or years. I can see the range within which a stock has traded and get an insight into the volatility of the stock concerned. This information will help me make decisions about the size of my position and my targets.

> **CHARTS ARE VALUABLE TOOLS WHEN MAKING INVESTMENT DECISIONS.**

Names to know: Charles Dow

Charles Dow (1851–1902) was the co-founder of the world's most important financial newspaper, The *Wall Street Journal*, in July 1889. In those days, companies did not have to file reports with the US Securities and Exchange Commission, so for the general public financial information was very hard to obtain. There were also no publications that showed stock prices on a daily basis, and the general public had no way of finding out what was going on in the financial markets. The *Wall Street Journal* changed all that.

Charles Dow, together with his colleague Edward Jones, was the first to create a number of indexes that represented the average performance of stocks. The first one, devised in 1884, is now called the Dow Jones Transportation Index, and the most important one, introduced in May 1896, is the Dow Jones Industrial Average.

When you follow the graph of the Dow Jones Industrial Average from the beginning, it is a lesson in history, and illustrates the impact of important events on the stock market. For example, at the start of the First World War in 1914, the New York Stock Exchange was closed for four months and the index could not be calculated. When it reopened four months later it was down 25%. You can also see all the bear and the bull markets that have existed over the last 110 plus years.

Charles Dow wrote a column in the WSJ called 'Review & Outlook', a title that still runs today. His column was full of investment lessons, such as: 'The public, as a whole, buys at the wrong time and sells at the wrong time. The average operator, when he sees two or three points profit, takes it; but, if a stock goes against him two or three points, he holds on waiting for the price to recover, with oftentimes, the result of seeing a loss of two or three points run into a loss of ten points.' I would say that this is as true today as it was over 100 years ago.

A very important school of technical analysis is called the Dow Theory, which says that all the information there is to know is already priced into the market. This is a key assumption in all the technical analysis that is in use today. Dow Theory talks about the importance of volume and trends, and tries to subdivide trends into three different time phases, from longer term to short term. Charles Dow formed the basis for technical analysis as we know it today.

▼ Technical analysis: points to remember

Let me summarise:

1. The first thing I do when looking at a stock is look at the charts to see the present level at which the stock is trading compared to its historical range. I don't just take one time period, I take several.

2. The second step is to try to determine whether the stock is ranging or trending. I do this by drawing trend lines (in my head or on paper).

3. The third step is to see if I can find a classic stock pattern and signs of divergence. I am looking to sell stocks towards the upper end of their range if they seem to have run out of steam. If less volume trades, a movement in the stock price is less significant than when this happens with a lot of volume.

Please remember that as far as I am concerned, analysing stock charts is just one part of the investment framework. If you use it in isolation it will sometimes work but it is not the way to build a proper investment portfolio.

▶ Part 6

Reality check

After you have completed all the analysis described in the previous sections, you might finally have come up with an idea that you want to invest in, and you will probably be keen to get going. However, this is the point where you need to sit back and look at the bigger picture. Ask yourself if the analysis really adds up, and answer a few questions, such as the ones below. Funnily enough, some of the answers might reinforce your opinion if you were thinking of shorting a stock.

▼ Q&A

Do I really want to invest in a company with an enormous pension deficit?

A company is responsible for ensuring that pensions are paid every month to its retired employees, and for this purpose they set up a pension fund. Some companies have insufficient assets in their pension fund to pay all the future retirees. This means the pension fund is in deficit. If you invest in a company that has a huge pension deficit, even though the underlying business is very profitable, it might be a very risky investment. The drag from the retirees could be just too large.

Do I really want to invest in a company that pays its executives huge bonuses?

As I have said previously, if management can pay itself whatever it wants and does not leave enough 'fat' for a rainy day, it seems pointless to invest in such a company. You'd be better off going elsewhere.

Do I really want to invest based on rumours?

Trading based on rumours and tips is often wrong and has no place in the life of a serious investor. You have to do the work before you invest – there are no shortcuts.

Do I really want to invest after a profit warning?

I have found profit warnings to be like buses, there might be none for a while, and then two or three come along at once. If you decide that a company is cheap after the first warning, that judgement is often based purely on the fact that the stock price is lower than it was before, without taking into account that management might have lost control of the relevant company, which could be followed by further warnings and an even lower stock price in the future.

Do I really want to invest in a rights issue?

A rights issue is one way for a company to raise money to strengthen its financial position. In a rights issue all existing shareholders are given the opportunity to buy more shares at a discount to the current stock price.

I don't like giving more money to companies. They usually need it because they are in serious trouble, or because they want to expand and buy other businesses. All too often, businesses that buy up other companies are doing it to hide the fact that their own business is no longer growing organically. Of course, management will not tell you this. They will say that there can be enormous synergies and cost savings by combining two different companies.

In theory, this is true, but in practice it can go seriously wrong. That is why businesses often go through cycles where they start as a good company, go on to buy other companies, then become too aggressive and too indebted, and then are forced to sell part of their conglomerate to raise money to pay off their debt. To me a rights issue is a huge warning sign.

Am I psychologically ready to trade?

Do I feel I can trade in a disciplined manner, or are there personal issues at work that will cause me to take unnecessary risks. (See Part 7.)

Do I really want to invest in a sector or stock that I lost money in the last few times that I traded?

The answer might well be no, because you obviously did not get it right the last time, so you might have no edge, i.e. you are not sufficiently in tune with this stock or sector to be able to make money. Also by continuing to go back this might become a personal fight between the specific stock and yourself, not ideal if you want to have a healthy trading mind.

Was my idea original enough?

It is fine to have some ideas in your portfolio that a lot of people are looking at, but you have to have enough original ideas to give the whole portfolio a nice balance.

This is in no way a complete list of the things you should be asking yourself – try to make your own.

▼ The next step

When I trade my aim is to maximise the chance that my decisions are the right ones. If you follow this framework you will be a much better trader. That doesn't mean you will always be right but you will be right more often. Risk management is the key to making sure you don't lose too much in those cases when you are wrong. Don't forget our first aim is to preserve capital and our second aim is to make money.

> THE BEST TRADERS ARE THOSE WHO ARE STREET SMART. THEY HAVE A SIXTH SENSE OF WHEN NOT TO TRADE.

▶ Part 7

Head check

You can read this book, learn and follow all the different technical and money management concepts, and still be a terrible trader. The reason for this is that you are a human being with a brain that might not always do what it should do or what you want it to do. This is totally normal but you can't make money without appreciating this properly. That is why I now want to discuss trading psychology.

▼ Finding the right balance

We already know that the market is unpredictable and that a rigid set of trading rules will not work. We are not robots with inbuilt microprocessors; instead we have real emotions, and we must therefore accept that psychological factors will impact on our trading performance.

In practice, this means that we have to control the two basic instincts of trading: greed and fear. On the one hand we want to be rich and successful, but on the other, we are frightened of losing what we have, and knowing we have to take risks if we want to make money. We have to get the balance right.

The smart way to trade is by doing the groundwork and by using the portfolio construction and risk management techniques described in Part 8. You will find that you are less likely to be dominated by greed or fear.

▼ An emotional roller coaster

It is easy to get used to making profits over time, but losses remain painful, no matter how much experience a trader has. As losses happen very frequently it can make life pretty tough. After a profitable day you don't go home on a high – it feels good, and sometimes it might even feel great. However, when you make a loss it feels terrible.

The risk spectrum

One of the managers I reported to at Goldman Sachs always used to say that everyone gets what they want from the market. What he meant was that some people love risk, and they invariably end up taking large positions, probably larger than they should. As these positions often go wrong, the careers of these traders are usually cut short. If they are lucky they might become rich, if not they might well end up with nothing.

There are also those at the opposite end of the spectrum. Some people are total perfectionists; they would rather make no decision than a wrong decision. I have seen many traders who are scared of their own shadow, and are so afraid of taking risk (in case it goes wrong), that putting on a new position for them becomes an all-but impossible task. These are the traders who are looking for confirmation that they would have been right in the first place. Unfortunately by the time they put on their trade, it is often too late, and the opportunity for profit has gone. Think about where you are on the spectrum: if you are a thrill seeker or a mouse, then sticking to the methodology of this book will be even more critical to your survival.

Trading is such a tiring job, with markets moving day and night, and unpredictable world events happening all the time. Even the best traders will lose money and suffer from exhaustion. You have to appreciate that this is a fact of life and accept it and work around it or you will never be a successful trader or investor.

THE PAIN OF LOSING IS FAR GREATER THAN THE JOY OF WINNING.

▼ 'Behavioural investing'

One name to watch in the field of market psychology is James Montier.

Using neuroscience as a starting point, Montier highlights two particular traits that are of significance to investors.

1. The first is that we are hard-wired for the short term. We find the chance of short-term gains very attractive. They appear to stimulate the emotional centres of the brain and release dopamine. This makes us feel confident, stimulated, and generally good about ourselves. It means we tend to take decisions faster than we should.

2. The second is that we appear to have a predisposition towards herding behaviour (in the same way as sheep). The pain of social exclusion (in the case of a trader, this means betting against everyone else) is felt in exactly the same part of the brain that feels real physical pain. Therefore, pursuing strategies that contradict the prevailing view, could be compared to having your arm broken on a regular basis. People don't mind being wrong, as long as other people are wrong as well.

COMMON MISCONCEPTION: Trading is fun

Trading is very difficult and very painful. You will be competing against the finest brains in the world. Mistakes are very costly. To succeed you need to be focused at all times. If you find that fun I do envy you. I find it tiring, frustrating and difficult. I see it as a necessary evil to protect my future wellbeing. For fun I rather go and watch a football game. Having said that, I do think that being able to manage your own finances and accepting responsibility for your own future, will give you enormous satisfaction.

It is very difficult to control these two impulses. Psychologists have found that self-control is a limited resource: the more we use it, the less we have left over for the next time it is required.

I believe that the best way to use trading psychology is to get to know yourself and guard against your weaknesses. You are often your own worst enemy. If you have a trading plan and a dose of self-discipline, this should help to ensure maximum chances of survival in the stock market. It might take you longer to get rich, but you would have to be pretty unlucky to lose all your money.

Keeping yourself in check
- You know less than you think you do.
- Try to focus on the facts, not the stories.
- More information isn't necessarily better information.
- Listen to those who disagree with you.
- Examine your mistakes, failures aren't just bad luck.
- You didn't know it all along, you just think you did.
- Do not take information at face value, think carefully about how it was presented to you.

('Keeping yourself in check' reproduced courtesy of James Montier.)

Also, making investment decisions in real life is very different to doing it in theory. In practice, the difference between making money

---

▷ Essential reading:
'Behavioural Investing' by James Montier

A strategist at GMO UK Ltd, James Montier has written the 'bible' in the field of the actual behaviour of players in the stock market. He tries to explain how markets operate in practice, as opposed to how they should operate in theory, and why this is the case. His work is usually backed up by robust scientific research.

and losing it, is often based on a decision one makes when the going gets really tough. If your trading plan was to sell a position after losing 10% of the money invested, but you are down 50% in one go when the market opens after the company issues a very bad profit warning, are you going to cut your position and lock in (realise) this loss? Sometimes the answer will be yes, sometimes it will be no – you are the one who will have to make that call.

This is what sets great traders apart – they tend to make better decisions when backed into a corner. However, all these great traders have a basic risk framework that ensures that they still have the ability to trade the next day, independent of what happens in the market. Mediocre traders will not stick to the most basic game plan – they will always find a reason not to.

Key traits of a good trader

Ability to listen	You learn more from listening to other people than continually talking yourself. Trading is one-dimensional: you either make money or you lose it. The prize goes to the person who makes money, not the one who talks the most.
Ability to analyse	You need to do many things before you trade. To go through all the steps and process all the information takes discipline and analytical ability.
Ability to realise when things don't add up	You might have done all the work and the trade looks good. However, there is this little voice in the back of your mind that tells you not to trade. I call it trader's instinct – it is often wise to listen. If it looks too good to be true, it probably is ...
Ability to sometimes be flexible and sometimes be stubborn	If you change your mind too often as a trader you will drive yourself mad. However, sometimes you just have to admit you are wrong, change your mind and move on.
Numerical skills	If you don't know the answer to 10 times 3 you will have a problem trading.

Names to know: George Soros

George Soros (1930–) was born in Budapest, Hungary, and survived both the Nazi and Soviet occupations in 1944 and 1946 respectively. He emigrated to England in 1947, and supported himself with work as a railway porter and waiter at Quaglino's restaurant, where he was once told that with hard work he might one day become head waiter. In fact, he graduated from the London School of Economics where his passion for the philosophy of Karl Popper was born, and he went on to secure an entry-level position with the merchant bank Singer & Friedlander.

He moved to New York in 1956, where he launched his financial career and his investment advisory firm Soros Fund Management, which would become the Quantum Fund. Under Soros the Quantum Fund famously generated an average annual return of more than 30%, and on two occasions returned investors over 100%.

He developed his theory of reflexivity for economics in his book *The Alchemy of Finance* (1987). It is a complex theory, but basically Soros believes that market prices find a way to influence the so-called fundamentals that are already supposed to be reflected in the market prices. When Internet stocks were doing well, the large quantities of money that were being invested changed the economics of this sector, and caused even more money to be pumped into it. There was no self-correcting mechanism, and according to Soros this is the normal state of affairs. When left alone markets tend to overshoot to either the upside or the downside. 'Stock market bubbles don't grow out of thin air. They have a solid basis in reality, but reality as distorted by a misconception.'

In 1987 Soros stopped actively managing the Quantum Fund and decided to turn his focus to philanthropy. He has since supported a wide range of projects throughout the world.

▼ Mental toughness

How do you find out if you are suited to trading? Steve Ward, a professional trader performance and psychology coach, and author of 'High Performance Trading', has tried to find out what types of traders are able to raise their game under pressure, and which ones start performing below their potential. One of his insights is that good traders are able to bounce back from losses and retain a certain amount of self-confidence: they have mental toughness.

▷ Test your mental toughness

There are five areas to address here:

1. Motivation

Are you trading for the right reasons? If your only reason to trade is to make money it probably will not work. You need to have an interest in financial markets and companies.

2. Self confidence

Do you believe in yourself? Would you still believe in yourself if everything was going wrong and you started losing money?

3. Focus

Are you focused? Trading requires total commitment; if you are busy doing other things you will find it hard to be successful.

4. Composure

Are you able to control your emotions? If you tend to panic, or get over-emotional, trading might not be for you ...

5. Resilience

Are you single-minded about achieving your goals? Trading is

The five components of mental toughness

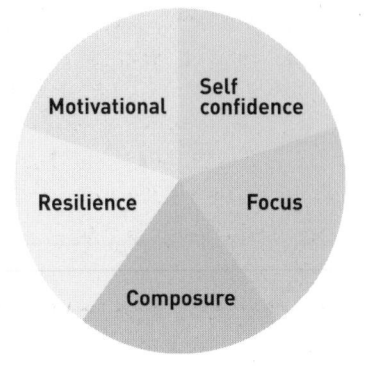

a painful occupation. You are often wrong and if you are not able to bounce back and try again it is not going to work ...

You need all five traits to be a good trader; four out of five is not enough. But even if you are unable to tick every box at the moment you now know what is required and what you need to work on.

Unfortunately, while all five are necessary to be a trader they do not necessarily mean you will be a successful one. You could be self-confident and resilient, focused and composed, and really want to be a trader – and yet you still might not make money. However, following the framework given in this book will help.

▶ ▶ The inside track
Women make better traders

A study by Barber and Odean (*Quarterly Journal of Economics*, Feb 2001) looked at the differences in trading between men and women. Having examined the trading accounts of 35,000 households, they found that men turn their portfolio over 0.77 times a year, while women have a holding period of almost two years (they turn over 0.53 times a year). So the average man trades almost 50% more frequently than the average woman. The next logical question is whether men trade more often because they have better analytical ability and thus come up with more good trading ideas. The research shows that this is not the case. The quality of the security selection is pretty similar between men and women. What they do find is that men, especially single men, are overconfident relative to women. Men pull the trigger quicker and trade having done less homework than single women; this leads to more frequent trading and higher transaction costs, and thus a lower return. It seems that getting married will make a man a better trader; conversely, female traders seem to become less profitable after they get married.

Names to know: Jesse Livermore

Jesse Livermore (1877–1940) is one of the most famous stock market traders of all time. Jesse was born on a farm in Massachusetts, and ran away from home at the age of 14.

His first job was posting stock quotes on the stock boards for brokerage firm Paine Webber. He quickly started getting a feel for how stock prices moved and started trading, initially in a very small way, for himself; later he would take positions as large as the local bucket shops (fraudulent brokerage firms) would let him. As the 'Boy Plunger' made more and more money, the bucket shops refused to trade against him any longer, and he moved to New York City where he began one of the most incredible careers as a securities speculator. His life is portrayed brilliantly in the book *Reminiscences of a Stock Operator* by Edwin Lefèvre, a must-read for every trader.

He was known as the 'Great Bear of Wall Street' after he made $3 million in the stock market crash known as the 'Panic' of 1907, and was worth $100 million after being short in the Wall Street Crash of 1929. He went on to lose his fortunes three times, and is said to have had bipolar disorder, which culminated in his suicide in 1940. The story that he had lost all his money by the time of his death is untrue. He was still worth over $5 million, a sizeable fortune.

Livermore was a high-momentum trader and believed that following large trends was what made money. One of his key talents was timing; he could successfully call the bottom of bear markets, and adopted a hold and wait strategy in bull markets, only to sell at the peak. He did not want to discuss what he was thinking with other people and did not want to hear their opinions. Whenever he broke this rule he would end up losing money. The cornerstone of his philosophy was to add to winning positions and cut losses quickly.

▷ Trader toughness self-assessment

Take a few moments to fill this out. When you are finished, check your answers in the evaluation section that follows, to determine your mental toughness, strengths and areas for improvement.

Answer 'T' for True or 'F' for False for each statement.

1.   I bounce back quickly from setbacks, losses, and errors ...
2.   It is easy for me to put losing trades behind me ...
3.   If I have a losing trade early on, it is hard for me to turn my performance around ...
4.   One or two losses or losing days does not shake my confidence ...
5.   I see slumps in my trading performance as temporary ...

6.   I trade at my best even under pressure ...
7.   I get too nervous and anxious when trading to perform at my full potential ...
8.   Sometimes I panic and make bad decisions under pressure ...
9.   I am able to execute my trading plan without hesitation ...
10.   I often find myself planning trades that I do not execute and executing trades that I did not plan ...

11.   My concentration and focus is excellent throughout the day ...
12.   I am rarely distracted when I am trading ...
13.   I am able to re-focus easily after a distraction, e.g. losing trade ...
14.   I focus mainly on my P&L (profits and losses) when trading ...
15.   I have clear routines and rituals that I stick to during the day/my trading ...

16.   I see myself as a successful trader ...
17.   I frequently worry about losing trades and losing money ...
18.   I know my strengths and weaknesses as a trader ...

19. I am frequently negative about my trading performance and myself ...
20. I am a disciplined trader ...
21. I love trading and find it enjoyable ...
22. I find myself just going through the motions a lot in trading ...
23. I have clear trading goals that are important for me to achieve ...
24. I know clearly why trading is important to me ...
25. I am a motivated trader ...

SCORING

Section 1, questions 1–5, deals with 'Resilience' or your ability to bounce back from setbacks and mistakes.
Score 1 point for each of the following answers:
1. T   2. T   3. F   4. T   5. T

Section 2, questions 6–10, deals with 'Composure' or the ability to handle pressure.
Score 1 point for each of the following answers:
6. T   7. F   8. F   9. T   10. F

Section 3, questions 11–15, deals with 'Focus' or your ability to concentrate.
Score 1 point for each of the following answers:
11. T   12. T   13. T   14. F   15. T

Section 4, questions 16–20, deals with your 'Self confidence' and the factors that affect confidence.
Score 1 point for each of the following answers:
16. T   17. F   18. T   19. F   20. T

Section 5, questions 21–25, deals with 'Motivation'.
Score 1 point for each of the following answers:
21. T   22. F   23. T   24. T   25. T

Interpretation: a score of 4 in any one of the five sections means that area is a strength; 2 or less highlights a weakness in that area that needs to be addressed.

Overall score
20–25: indicates strength in overall mental toughness
13–19: indicates an average to moderate skill in mental toughness and you would benefit from specifically targeted mental skills work.
12 or below: means that you need to up your mental game.

(Test reproduced courtesy of Steve Ward.)

▼ Check before you trade

So what does this all mean in practice? I think you need to be aware that you and everyone else who trade stocks have inbuilt weaknesses that affect behaviour. Be aware that most people's natural predisposition is to trade as part of the herd.

There is not a lot you can do about other people's behaviour, other than accepting that stock prices are often irrational, and try to take advantage when this is the case. You should control your own behaviour though. Try and find out where you fall short and seek to improve. When you have other things on your mind the answer is normally to trade smaller positions than usual for a while. Everybody suffers from periods of low confidence and lack of motivation. That's okay but it is not okay to ignore it. Keep yourself in check and remind yourself of the key traits of good traders. Always have a quick think about your psychological wellbeing before you put on a new trade.

▶Part 8

Building your portfolio and controlling its risks

By now you hopefully have a reasonable understanding of how to find an investment idea and how to analyse it, from a historical, fundamental and a technical point of view. In this section I will discuss how to ensure that you put the right amount of money into each idea, how to balance those ideas, and what to do when things go wrong. I will also explain a few concepts that you need to understand in order to achieve this. Some have been explained to a certain extent in earlier sections, but it doesn't hurt to repeat them, as they are essential to trading and investing.

▼ Risk versus reward

Obviously, you only want to put on a trade if the odds are in your favour. Let's say chemical products company A was trading at £4.20 last week. Over the weekend it was the target of a take-over bid by chemicals company B at £5.00, and chemical company A is now trading at £5.05. Your view is that a third company will come in and bid £5.50. You might believe this because you have looked at the industry and believe that the third company probably would not allow the other two companies to get together as it would create too strong a competitor in the chemicals industry. So you have two possible outcomes if you were to buy the stock at £5.05: you either lose 5p or you make 45p.

If you think the odds of either situation are about 50:50 you have a 9:1 reward versus risk ratio. That is much higher than you would probably have in reality, but if that's your view, then the stock is clearly mispriced at £5.05. As a general principle I think you should be looking for a reward to risk ratio of at least 3:1. Always think of how much you are potentially risking before you make a trade. If you are prepared to lose 50p on a trade it doesn't make sense to put on the trade if you can only make 25p.

▼ Stop losses:
run your winners, cut your losers

The logical conclusion of the above is that if you are prepared to lose 50p you should be aiming for a profit of at least £1.50 on the trade. Or the other way around, if you have a trade where you hope to make 75p you should cut your position if the price drops 25p below the purchase price; this is called a stop loss.

Stop loss

A level of the stock price where the stock position is liquidated. The goal is to contain further losses.

Most people have great difficulty selling a stock below the price at which they bought it. Let's say a company announces it will not be able to make as much money as the market expected. An unexpected profit warning can make any stock drop dramatically. After this happens most people just do nothing, and pray for the stock to go up: 'If only my stock would go back up to where I bought it I would be so happy.' A cynic would say that investors in the stock market pray more than people in real places of worship.

It is important to realise that it is not just okay to sell a stock when you are losing money, it is in fact essential if you want to survive. It is too easy to spend time watching the stocks that are making you money, while losing sight of the ones that are making a loss. In fact most people sell out of profitable positions much too early just to lock in that profit. There is a stock market saying that you can't go broke taking a profit, but if you forget about cutting your losers, you probably will end up broke anyway.

Good traders cut their losers and run their winners. Even if you are right only half the time, if you run your winners and cut your losers, keeping to the 3:1 rule will ensure that you make money.

COMMON MISCONCEPTION: derivatives are a great way to enhance returns and reduce risk

Trading complex financial instruments known as derivatives will remove some risks, but will introduce others that you never knew even existed. You can buy an option on a stock that will make money if a stock goes down (a put option), however, if the person who sold you that put goes bankrupt, what happens to the put option? Will you get paid or will you have to speak to the administrator? In 2003 legendary investor Warren Buffet described derivatives as time bombs and 'financial weapons of mass destruction', that could harm the whole economic system. How right he was.

I would suggest that beginners, as well as more experienced people, steer clear of options and futures. There is only a small group of professionals that makes money from options and this is because these traders are often able to buy at low prices and sell at high prices. That is where the money is made, not necessarily in the product itself.

To quote Buffet: 'Traders and company management love using derivatives. They are almost impossible to value leading to 'marking errors' [giving a product a price that doesn't reflect its true value]. I can assure you that the marking errors in the derivatives business have not been symmetrical. Almost invariably, they have favored either the trader who was eyeing a multi-million dollar bonus or the CEO who wanted to report impressive "earnings" (or both). The bonuses were paid, and the CEO profited from his options. Only much later did shareholders learn that the reported earnings were a sham.'

Derivatives serve a purpose as a hedging instrument or to enhance returns, but my view is that if you are worried about stock risk just reduce your position or liquidate it, but leave derivatives to someone else.

▼ Hedging

You might really like a stock, but are worried about the market, and you are looking to hedge your risk. The way to proceed is to buy the stock, but to sell the market (through an Exchange Traded Fund (ETF), as discussed in Chapter 1, for example) against it as protection.

You might not want to hedge pound for pound though, for example, you might have bought £2,000 of stock A, and sell £1,000 of FTSE 100 ETF against it (this is called a hedge ratio or 'delta' of 50%).

Or maybe you like a stock but are not sure about the rest of the sector. In that case, you can hedge by selling a sector ETF, or by going short a few individual names in the same sector. So, for example, if you like mining company Rio Tinto and want to buy £2,000 of stock for a company specific reason, but you are worried about the mining sector overall, you could short £1,000 of BHP Billiton and short £1,000 of Xstrata.

Going long Barclays and short Royal Bank of Scotland is another example, this is also known as a pair trade.

Pair trades are not for the faint hearted, and you really have to know what you are doing, and why you are doing it. You can also use a sector ETF for this purpose if one side of the pair is too daunting.

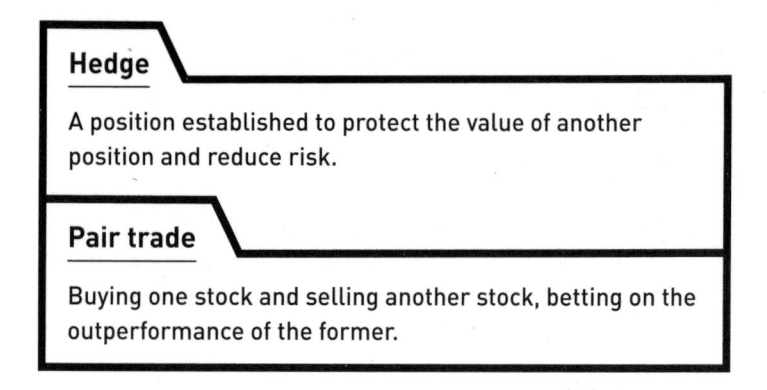

Hedge

A position established to protect the value of another position and reduce risk.

Pair trade

Buying one stock and selling another stock, betting on the outperformance of the former.

> **COMMON MISCONCEPTION:** the smartest person makes the most money

In 1994 there was a hedge fund called Long Term Capital Management (LTCM). It employed Nobel Prize winners, Myron Scholes and Robert Merton, and was run by John Meriwether, a hugely successful former head of bond trading at Salomon Brothers, which was later taken over by Citibank. This trio of seriously smart financial brains specialised in well-thought-out, low-risk trades. In 1998 LTCM blew up, wiping out all the capital of the investors, which just goes to show that you can be the smartest guys in the world and still not beat the market. On a moral note, if you believe in justice, you won't find it here: both Scholes and Meriwether are again running large funds.

Luck can play a big role in the stock market; a lucky person will always make more money than a prudent investor (at least in the short term when the luck has not yet run out). This is probably the most frustrating thing about trading. You can do everything according to the book, and only make a small amount of money, while another person with no knowledge can risk everything, get lucky, and end up very wealthy. During my career I have seen people make money and then lose it all again. My suggestion is to play the long-term, careful game. As far as luck is concerned, over the long term its role becomes much smaller.

▼ Gross and net exposure

Your portfolio will consist of some stocks that you believe are going to go up and probably some that you believe will go down or that you want to use to hedge your long exposure. Let's say you have capital of £10,000. Assume you have stocks worth £3,000 on the long side and stocks that are worth £2,000 on the short side. The rest is in cash. Your net exposure is long £1,000 (long minus short), your gross exposure is £5,000 (long plus short).

▼ Leverage

Most brokers will allow you to borrow money from them to invest in the stock market. You may have to put up just £10,000 to be able to own £50,000 worth of stocks: this is called five-to-one leverage. This sounds enticing, but unfortunately it tends to be expensive and when it goes wrong, it goes really wrong really fast: if you are 20% wrong you will lose all your money; if you are 30% wrong you will end up owing the broker a lot of money. My view is that you should never use leverage, and that you should always invest very conservatively.

▼ Money management rules

One of the hardest things about investing is managing your portfolio. You need to make sure you put the right amount of money in each stock and balance the portfolio carefully; it will need constant maintenance and adjustment. This is something most professionals struggle to get right.

Let me give you a set of money management rules that I feel comfortable with myself. You do not need to copy it exactly but it is a pretty good list. It is also key to be consistent in setting rules and following them. Bad traders often have rules as well but they just keep breaking them.

Note that these are money management rules, which you need to control your investment portfolio, rather than trading rules, which I told you to be wary of as they can lead to disaster when the investment environment changes, and the rules stop working. Money management rules work much more consistently through different and changing investment climates.

1. Never be long more than 50%
If you have £10,000 of cash never own ('be long') stocks to a value of more than £5,000 at any time.

2. Never be short more than 50%
If you have £10,000 of cash never sell (without owning i.e. 'be short') stocks valued worth more than £5,000 at any time.

3. No leverage
Don't use more money than you have. Combining this with rules 1 and 2 means you can be long £7,500 of stocks and short £2,500 of stocks at a given period (or short £7,500 and long £2,500 and every combination in between – so that you are never more than £5,000 short or long at any time), but if your portfolio is larger it will require leverage – not something you should consider.

4. Never put more than 3% of your capital in one stock
Do not put all your eggs in one basket in case you drop it: I would suggest never put more than 3% in any single stock.

5. Never put more than 10% of your capital in one sector or in one thematic trade
There are many different sectors in the market; look for ideas elsewhere once you have put 10% of your money in one sector. Even if you are wrong on a certain sector, you are still in the game. And if you are right, you will make plenty anyway. Don't build your portfolio around one single idea such as the credit crunch – it is too risky and too lazy. You can do better than that.

6. Low conviction ideas and volatile stocks should have smaller positions than high conviction ideas and stable stocks
As a beginner the concept of ranking your ideas according to conviction and investing more money in those that are ranked highest, is not an easy one to grasp, but it is a skill worth developing. I would suggest the following capital allocation limits:

a. High conviction stocks 3%
b. Medium conviction 2%
c. Low conviction 1%
d. No conviction 0%

Highly volatile stocks (i.e. stocks that move a lot as discussed on pp.139–141) should have smaller position sizes.

7. Cut your losses
There is no debate about having to cut your losses, the question is at what level you will do this. Set this level before you do the

trade and never change it. There is always an excuse for not cutting but please do it anyway.

I have already discussed the 3:1 rule, where you do not trade unless you expect your potential profit to be three times higher than the associated risk. Set your stop by dividing the gain you hope to make by three to calculate the maximum acceptable level of loss. For example, when you buy a stock at £2.00 and aim to make 60p, you should cut when the stock starts trading under £1.80. You can use technical analysis to set realistic targets and stop losses.

It is not always easy to look at your trades like that. That is why I would suggest that the level to cut your trades when things go wrong should be somewhere between 5% and 10%. You can do this for each stock or for the whole portfolio. If you trade the portfolio as one big instrument, once the portfolio as a whole has lost 5%, you might consider getting rid of all investments and stop trading for a while to rethink. If you look at it on a stock-by-stock basis you may well have a higher tolerance of perhaps 10% (it can also be different per stock dependent on how volatile a stock is or on how big the position is).

8. Run your winners

The correct way to do this when the stock goes in your favour is to play defence; you don't want to find yourself in a situation where your stock is up 50% and you give it all back. If you buy the stock at 10, maybe set your initial cut at 9, and as the stock moves up increase your stop. For example, if the stock goes to 11, put your stop at 10 so you know this trade will never become a losing trade. When it goes to 12 put it at 11 and protect your 10% return – now that is trading the way I want you to do it!

9. Don't forget there is a world out there that impacts on your portfolio

You must be aware that rules change and that the world changes. You can have great ideas but if they are not working there are reasons for that. It can be because you have made mistakes, but

> **COMMON MISCONCEPTION:** penny shares are a real investment vehicle
>
> I have never been a fan of investing in stocks that cost a few pence instead of a few pounds.
>
> Let's say a company's market value is £5 million and it has 100 million shares outstanding. That means one share is worth 5p. If that same company had one million shares outstanding each share is worth £5. It is still the same company you are buying, independent of the absolute level of the share price. The fact that a share is 5p does not make it a better investment. In fact, I think it is a worse investment as the bid-offer spread (the difference between buying and selling price), is much bigger for the 5p stock than for the 500p stock. In the 5p stock you could easily lose 10% of your money between buying and selling without the stock price even moving, as the difference between where you can sell in the market versus where you can buy might well be 0.5p.
>
> People tend to invest in these stocks because there is often a good story attached to them. Perhaps the company has developed an amazing new technology that turns water into energy, and only a small investment is needed to see it through the next year, before it gets bought by one of the world's leading utilities. Or it could be the next telecom venture of an entrepreneur who made a fortune in his previous business. Or it could be a business that is about to go bankrupt, but which has one valuable asset that on its own is worth twice the share price. My advice is don't waste your time and steer clear.

it might also have been outside your control. For example, investors started taking a lot of money out of hedge funds at the end of 2008. You might have come up with some great strategies, but if they were similar to the ones held by those hedge funds who were forced to liquidate because of redemptions, you would have lost money no matter how good the rationale for your positions. That's why you need to know what else is going on in the world. This is another reason why fundamental analysis on its own is not sufficient to make money consistently. When you realise that other people are unwinding positions that you think make great trading opportunities, I am not suggesting that you shouldn't touch it, I am saying be aware of it and size your position in such a way that demonstrates you have taken all the risks into account.

10. Keep a trading diary

It is so easy to forget your reasoning for a trade you put on two weeks ago. Keeping a diary will remind you and be instructive. It will force you to write down why you think a trade is a good one and what size it should be. It will force you to put in writing the level at which you will cut your position and where you want to take profits. You will have to be honest with yourself and that is probably one of the most important skills in trading.

11. Do not break any stock exchange rules

You have to make sure that you only trade on information that is available to all other investors. If you know the director of a company, and he tells you something that might influence the price of the stock, do not trade. See the FSA website for more information.

▼ It's all about odds

I want to talk a bit about statistics here but if you are not a rocket scientist don't worry. It is only those statistics that are intuitive

Alpha
Profit made on a stock because you picked the right stock and the right sector.

Beta
Profit made on a stock because you picked the right market direction.

and that you might want to think about when building a portfolio. Remember, every time you trade you are playing the odds, i.e. you are using statistics in any case, so it might be worth reading on.

▷ The Greeks were ahead of the game

Let's say you are long a stock that goes up 12%, while the market goes up 5%. Of the 12% you made, 5% was due to you being long when the market went up. This is not due to your stock picking skills, it is only because you were long when the market went up. This 5% is called the beta. You must not think that this has no value – you were long and the market went up. That is better than being long when the market goes down! The other 7% return is due to your stock picking skills (not due to luck I am sure!). This can be divided into a sector component and a stock specific component, and both these components can be called alpha. Not everyone tends to view it this way but as far as I am concerned you cannot run a portfolio without thinking about alpha and beta.

Thinking in terms of alpha and beta will help you determine whether you make your money in a stock because you are a good stock picker, because you chose a stock in the right sector, or because the market went up and you got lucky.

In general I would say that over 50% of a stock's returns are due to movements in the overall market. If the market goes up most stocks do well and vice versa. This proves how important it is to

> **ONLY IF YOU HAVE GOOD REASON TO BELIEVE THAT AN INDIVIDUAL COMPANY WILL DO WELL SHOULD YOU ACCEPT THE SINGLE STOCK RISK.**

analyse the market direction properly. Another 25% is determined by sector performance. This means that you really have to think of macro factors affecting the whole industry before you invest in a stock in that sector. Only 25% of returns is due to the stock being a great company. So if you look at a company in isolation the odds of making money are not really in your favour.

By buying a stock, as opposed to buying the overall market or a whole sector through an exchange-traded fund, one adds a lot of individual stock risk. If you like banks, it might be better to buy a basket of five or ten banks than one specific bank, because if you pick the wrong bank you could lose a lot of money while the rest of the sector is doing well. So before you buy a stock you need to think about why you are buying that particular stock. For example, maybe you believe the stock market is going up. In that case buy an index ETF such as the FTSE 100. Or maybe you think banks are going to do well. In that case buy a bank ETF.

▷ Volatility

Before you can build a portfolio you also need to understand the concept of volatility. It takes a bit of statistical insight to understand

Volatility

The amount that a stock has typically moved over the past time period. It is often used to predict the risk of the stock over a future time period.

volatility but basically volatile stocks move around more than stocks that are less volatile. If your portfolio consists of only three stocks, all of them volatile, it will be much riskier than if it contains 20 stable companies.

Volatility is typically expressed in an absolute number or a percentage. Let's say the stock price is £1.00 and the volatility is 1% or 1p per day. In statistical terms this means that the stock price will close between 99p and £1.01 on the next trading day in 65% of cases. Usually volatility is expressed in annual terms. To go from a daily number of 1% to an annual number you multiply by 16 (don't ask me to explain this – that's the way statistics works). What it implies for the stock is that with a daily volatility of 1% and thus an annual volatility of 16% this stock will close within £0.84 and £1.16 in two out of every three years.

If you know the volatility of your portfolio, you have an indication of how much you can expect to gain or lose over the next day or year. It is too complicated to discuss how to calculate it for the purposes of this book, but your broker might do this for you, or be able to provide you the tools with which to do it. If they can't do it then maybe you should change broker.

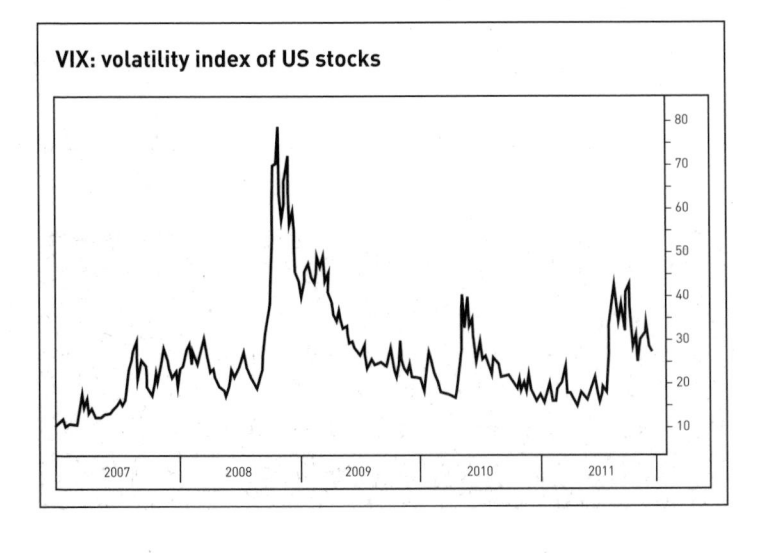

VIX: volatility index of US stocks

Volatility has its own index called VIX, which is shown in the chart above. This chart shows the unprecedented volatility of late 2008 with levels reached of 80% annualised. This means that most of the time a typical stock would move up to 5% per day. The latter part of the chart shows a volatility of 30% annualised or 2% per day. This is still very high given that normal annual volatility has historically been below 20%.

▷ Correlation

If the individual stocks you own are more volatile your portfolio will also be more volatile. However, the risk of your portfolio also depends on the correlation between the stocks in this portfolio.

Mining stock A will be more correlated to mining stock B than to food retailer A. If you only own mining stocks your portfolio will be more risky than if you have a diverse and balanced portfolio. Adding more stocks and sectors to your portfolio will reduce the risk of the portfolio. If there is less correlation between the different stocks, the more likely it is that your portfolio will be less volatile, and your returns more stable. And that means you will be able to sleep at night.

Correlation

A measure of the similarity between stocks.

VOLATILITY CAN HURT. BUT IT CAN HELP AS WELL. TAKE ADVANTAGE OF VOLATILITY WITH LIMIT BUY OR SELL ORDERS AT GREAT LEVELS JUST IN CASE IT GETS THERE.

▼ Trading in different markets

When building a portfolio it is a good idea to have as many strings to your bow as possible. Here we look at two more sectors that you might consider investing in to spread your risk: currency trading and commodities.

▼ Currency trading

At its most basic level, when you bet on a currency, you bet on the economic success of a country. The theory is that if a country does well economically, there will be a high demand for its currency and the value of the currency will go up. Conversely, if a country struggles economically, capital will leave the country looking for better returns, taking the value of the currency down with it. So it is all about capital flows – the demand and supply of a certain currency. When a currency goes down in value it is known as depreciation. Sometimes one currency is fixed against one or more other currencies, which, for example, is the case with the Hong Kong dollar (HKD) versus the US dollar. If the monetary authorities decide that the exchange rate is too high they might lower it, which is called a devaluation.

Currency trading is probably one of the most common short- (and long-) term trading strategies available to retail traders. Everybody seems to have a view on the direction that the dollar, the pound, or any other currency, might move. And it is relatively straightforward to open a trading account and back those views up with real money.

I am a big fan of currency trading for two reasons. First, it is such a great way to play macro-economic themes: basically for every macro theme there is a corresponding currency bet to take. Second, you are not just limited to the major currencies, such as the US dollar (USD) or the euro, as you will see later in this chapter.

Let's look at different currency plays by using a number of themes:

1. Commodities
2. Oil
3. Asia
4. Euro-zone break-up
5. Safe haven currencies
6. Carry trades
7. Pegged currencies
8. Quantitative easing

1. Commodities

As China has undergone a historically unparalleled phase of fixed investment in infrastructure and housing, there has been an enormous need for basic commodities such as iron ore and copper. China itself has not able to provide for its own needs and thus has had to import these commodities from other countries such as Australia, Canada and Brazil. This has lead to huge demand for currencies such as the Australian dollar (AUD), the Canadian dollar (CAD) and the Brazilian real (BRL), which have all showed significant strength over the last 10 years as you can see in the charts below.

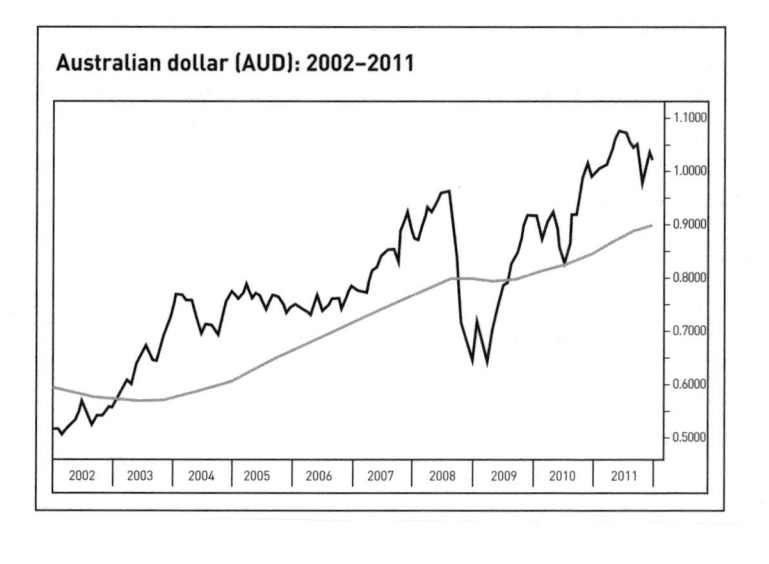

Australian dollar (AUD): 2002–2011

These charts can be confusing, but this one says that the AUD was worth 0.5 USD in 2002 and about 1 USD at the end of 2011. So the AUD doubled in value against the USD over this period.

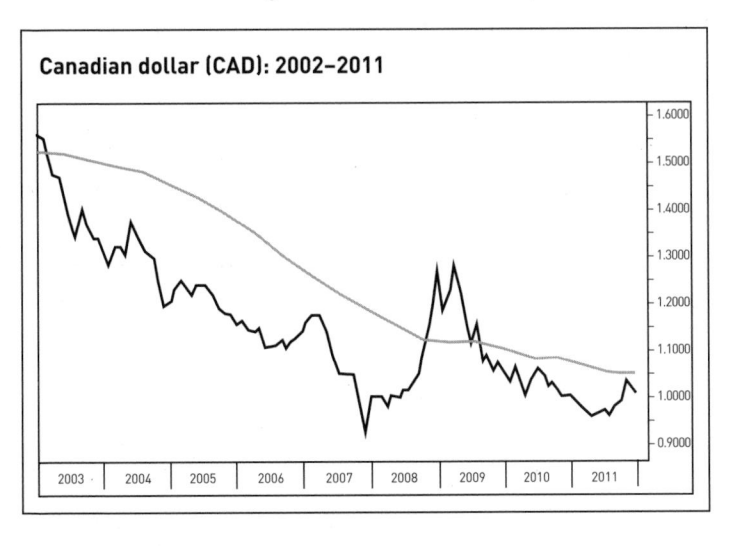

At the start of 2002 you needed 1.6 CAD to buy 1 USD, and in December 2011 there was virtual parity between the two currencies.

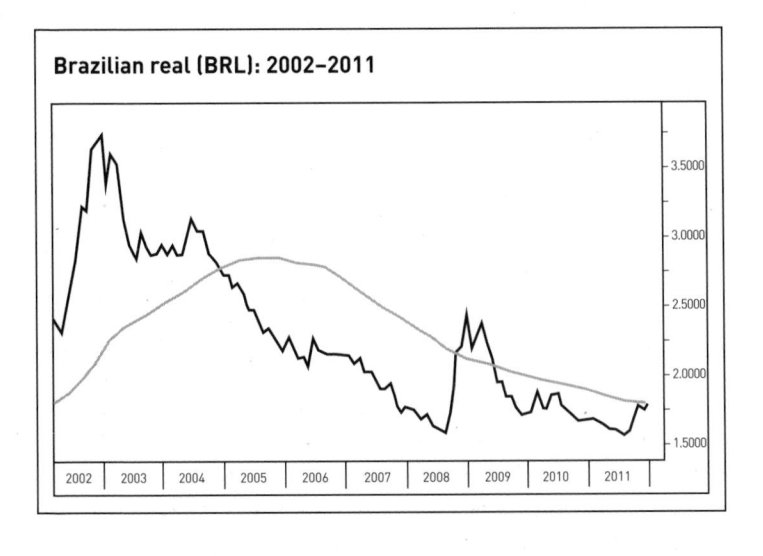

In 2003, 3.5 Brazilian reals bought 1 USD in 2003, and in December 2011 the USD is valued at 1.75 reals.

These charts are all against the USD, which has clearly showed significant weakness over this period (partially for its own reasons) and they all demonstrate how a lot of money can be made by being invested in the right currency at the right time.

Let's say you believe that the Chinese economy is going to slow down, then this could have massive implications for the country's commodity needs. This would make countries that export to China take a huge financial hit. Shorting these commodity currencies could be your 'China slowdown' play.

The chart below plots copper against the AUD since 2001. Pretty strong correlation I would say ...

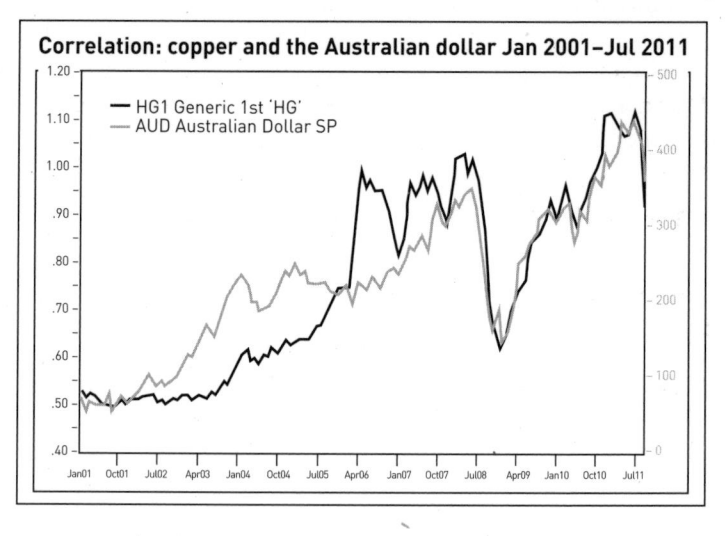

Correlation: copper and the Australian dollar Jan 2001–Jul 2011

There are also a number of other commodity currencies such as the South African rand and the Russian ruble. Again, this might help your ability to put a view on certain commodities into an actual trading or investment position. Some can also be regarded as a bit of a play on the gold price too, like the even more exotic Peruvian nuevo sol, due to the country's significant gold mining industry. However, be cautious as this is not a very liquid currency, i.e. it is not as easy to trade at a competitive price. The Brazilian real is not only a play on hard commodities but also on soft commodities such as soybeans and sugar, which again Brazil exports to China amongst others on a massive scale.

A good source of information for any country you might be interested in is the CIA factbook. This can be found online at https://www.cia.gov/library/publications/the-world-factbook/index.html.

2. Oil
If you are bullish on oil prices then Norway might be the country to back. About half of Norwegian exports are from the petroleum sector, which means that, in theory, higher oil prices should benefit the Norwegian krone (NOK). I say 'in theory' because in practice there are of course many other factors affecting the Norwegian economy besides the oil price, which in turn will affect the level of the NOK.

In addition, don't forget that every currency is quoted against another currency as a currency pair. So while something could be good for one currency, something else might be even better for another currency, thereby producing downward pressure on the (relative) exchange rate.

3. Asia
As mentioned above, China has been going through an exceptional period of growth, which has very much helped the 'commodity' countries. However, it has also been very beneficial for economic growth in other countries in the region, such as South Korea which itself is not a large commodity exporting country but much more an industrial product exporting country, with more than 25% of its exports going to China. This is why the Korean won (KRW) has been highly correlated with the economic fortunes of China, and indirectly with the strength of the commodity currencies.

However, it is important to realise how vulnerable these Asian currencies can be to internal shocks such as the Asian crisis in 1997–98, when the won halved against the USD, and similarly to external shocks after the Lehman bankruptcy in 2008 when it fell almost as much.

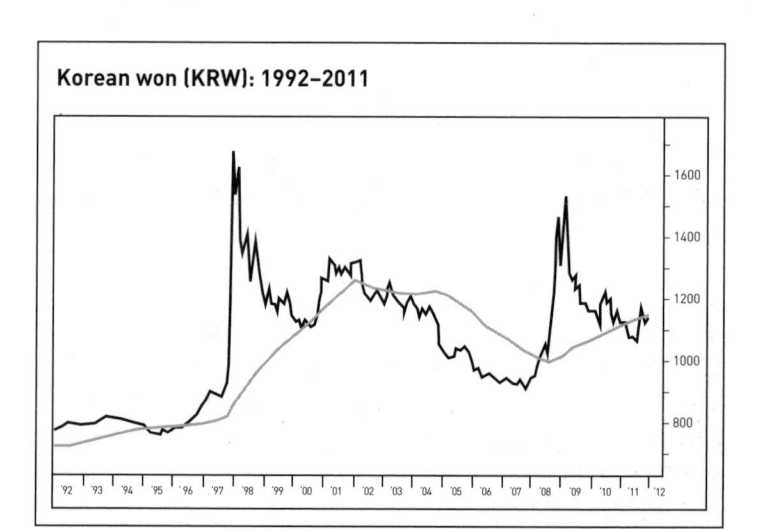

Korean won (KRW): 1992–2011

4. Euro-zone break-up

The euro came into existence on 1 January 1999, replacing currencies such as the German mark, the French franc and the Dutch guilder. The single currency worked really well for some countries like Germany, but not so well for others, including Spain and Italy.

If your view now is that the euro will not survive then a straight forward way of doing this might be to short the euro. However one has to be very careful because there could be some unintended consequences by being short the euro if the Euro-zone were to actually break up. This is because if you were short euros with a German bank they might want you to pay back in the strong new German mark, while if you are short with a Spanish bank or broker, you might well only need to pay back in weak Spanish pesetas. So make sure you read the small print of the place where you trade.

Anyway, one euro bought 0.9 USD in 2001 and 1.35 USD at the height of the European crisis in November/December. So late 2011, despite never ending news stories of the end of the euro, it did not seem to be apparent in the exchange rate of the euro against the USD ...

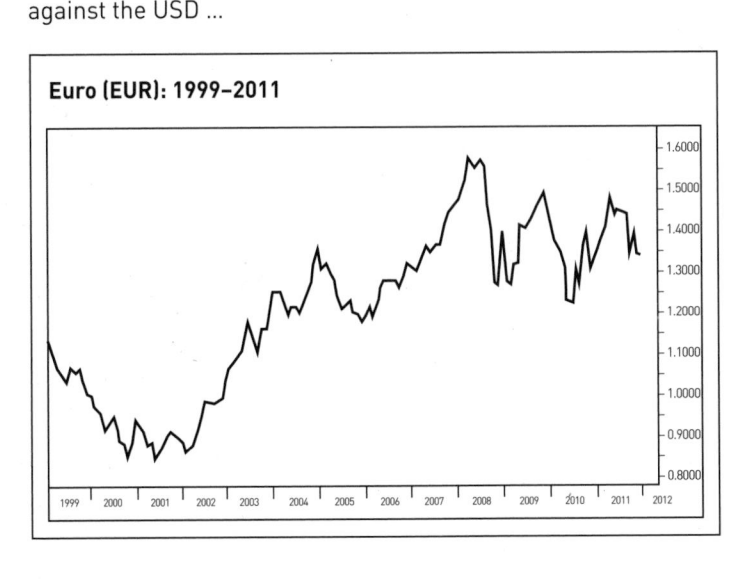

Euro (EUR): 1999–2011

5. Safe haven currencies

Three currencies stand out to me as safe haven currencies: the US dollar (USD), the Swiss franc (CHF), and the Singapore dollar.

US dollar: The USD is of course the major reserve currency in the world, making up 60–70% of the average government foreign exchange reserves. When things go wrong in the world people tend to flee to the USD. For example, when Lehman Brothers went down in 2008, money left all the currencies that had been strong up to that point, such as the commodity and Asian currencies, and moved into the USD (see KRW chart). It did not matter that the US stock market fell as fast as other global stock markets, the US currency was still seen as the safe haven in times of crisis. I don't think this is any different today than it was then.

Swiss franc: Another safe haven currency is the Swiss franc (CHF). It has also done very well historically in times of trouble. However, whereas the USD has recently seen almost unlimited printing by the Federal Reserve, with the resulting erosion in its value, this has not been the case in Switzerland. The result has been a massive rise in the level of the CHF against the USD and the euro. This 'appreciation' of the CHF versus the euro, has weakened the economic position of Switzerland, as Europe (and especially Germany) is its main trading partner. The result of this we will discuss further as part of the 'peg theme' below.

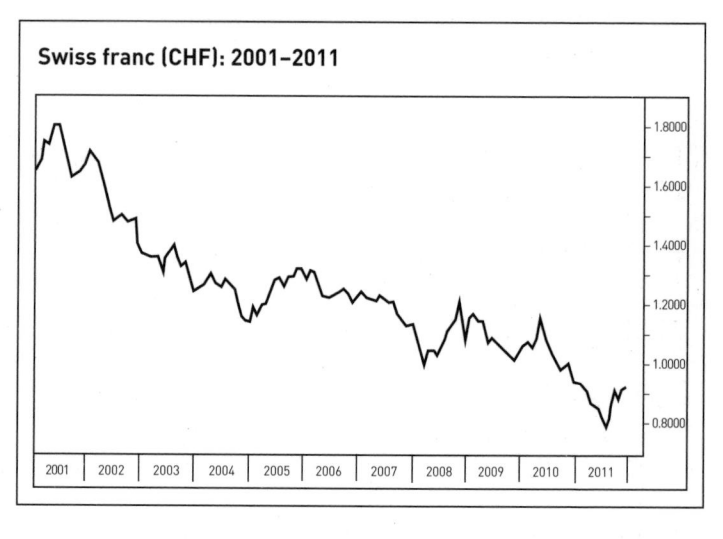

Swiss franc (CHF): 2001–2011

Singapore dollar: Singapore is a country that is seen as financially very well managed and politically very stable and is also a gateway into Asia and its economies. It is seen as the Asian Swiss franc, and in a world that feels very risky but where you still might want exposure to Asia, this might be a good currency to own. However, it is important to be aware that if the Asian economy turns sour, the safe haven effect of the Singapore dollar will probably be outweighed by the capital retreat back into the USD.

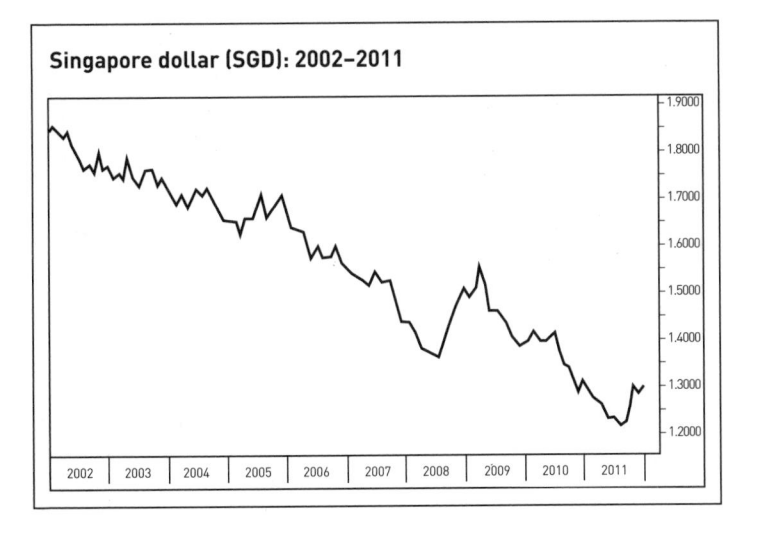

Singapore dollar (SGD): 2002–2011

6. Carry trades

The idea of a carry trade is to take advantage of an interest rate differential between different currencies.

For example, at the end of 2011 the one-year interest rate on the AUD was about 3.5%, while the one-year rate on the Japanese yen (JPY) was almost zero. This means that you can buy Australian dollars and receive 3.5% more per year than you need to pay out on the Japanese yen that you borrow. Brokers often let clients borrow money so they can do this in much larger size (leverage). So if you leveraged this ten times you could make over 30% (that is if the AUD does not weaken versus the yen). If you believe that Australia will keep growing over the next year (probably a bet on China) then this cross-currency trade might be something you want to do.

However as shown in the chart below, carry trades come with a huge health warning as they tend to be massively leveraged consensus positions with everybody doing the same thing, and when they go wrong they can go spectacularly wrong. In the Lehman crisis in 2008, there was an enormous amount of forced leveraged selling and the carry trade lost eight years worth of performance in less than one year, before reverting back into the previous direction. So basically the carry trade works very well when the economy performs well but when the economy slows or there is an external shock these trades often stop working.

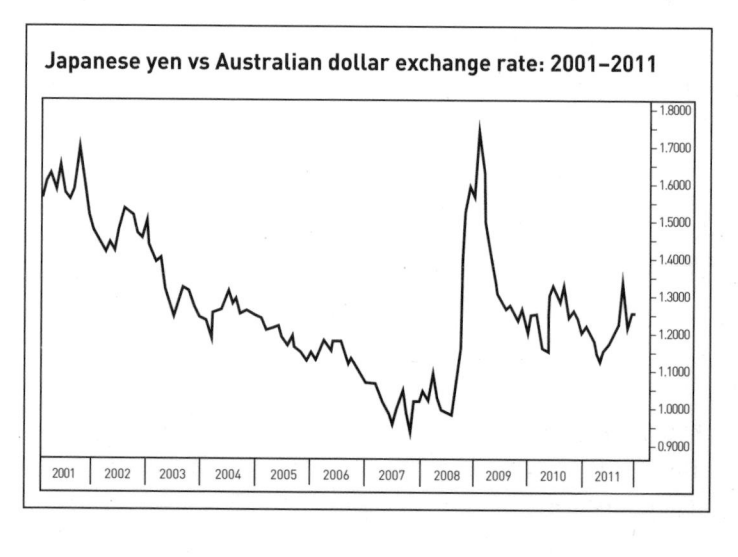

Japanese yen vs Australian dollar exchange rate: 2001–2011

7. Pegged currencies

If too much money enters a country it can potentially destroy the local economy because the price of its exports are forced up and internationally it becomes very uncompetitive.

As discussed before, one example of this has been Switzerland, which saw an enormous inflow of money into the country because of its safe haven status. People who did not trust the USD or the euro saw it as a good place to park their money. The result of this was that the Swiss National Bank decided to intervene to protect the domestic economy and weaken the CHF 'artificially' by threatening to print an unlimited amount of its currency to ensure it would be 'pegged' to a fixed rate of not worse than 1.20 CHF per euro. In this case the market decided to take the SNB at its word, and the bank did not have to sell much into the market to lower the value of the CHF to the desired rate.

As mentioned before the Hong Kong dollar (HKD) is pegged to the USD. With the Hong Kong economy doing so much better than the

US economy over the past 10 years this has really helped Hong Kong keep its currency at a much lower international level than it should have been. This caused a massive domestic investment boom with artificially low interest rates causing for example house prices to rise way more than if they had had a floating currency regime. Not nice if you like to buy a place to live. If your view is that the authorities might get rid of the peg at some point in the near future then buying the HKD could be a great trade. Of course timing a trade like that is incredibly hard and has cost a lot of people a lot of money.

Hong Kong dollar (HKD): pegged to USD during 2000–2002, and then pegged with a less than 1% trading band

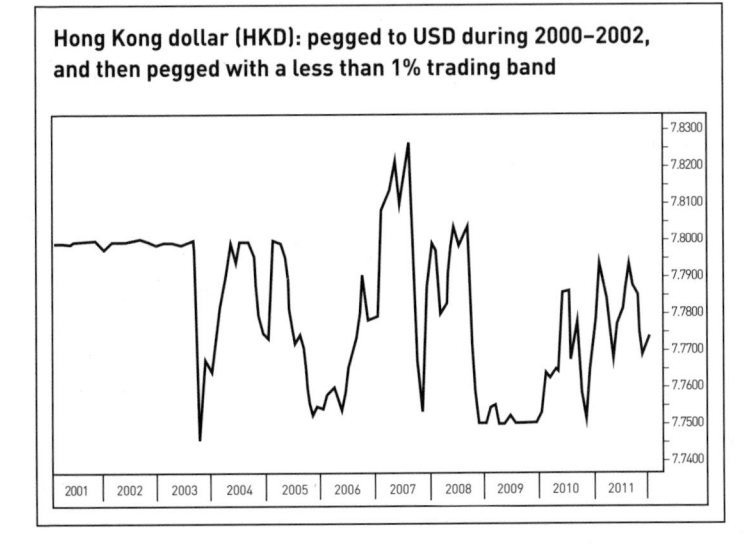

8. Quantitative easing

The USD is the king of all currencies. It holds a unique position as the main reserve currency, which means it is held as a storage of value outside the US as well. This is a great situation for the US, as its value is determined by more than just the relative economy versus the rest of the world, as other nations such as China are likely to always want to own some of it under pretty much any circumstances. What it means in practice is that the US tends to live beyond its natural means. However, as a trader there is no value judgment attached to this; all you need to do is understand the dynamics.

The best way to get an idea of the value of the USD is to plot it against a basket of other major world currencies, as opposed to just one currency, which is more commonly known as the DXY.

The chart below shows that the USD has lost enormous ground versus other currencies over the past 10 years, something which we saw before against many different individual currencies.

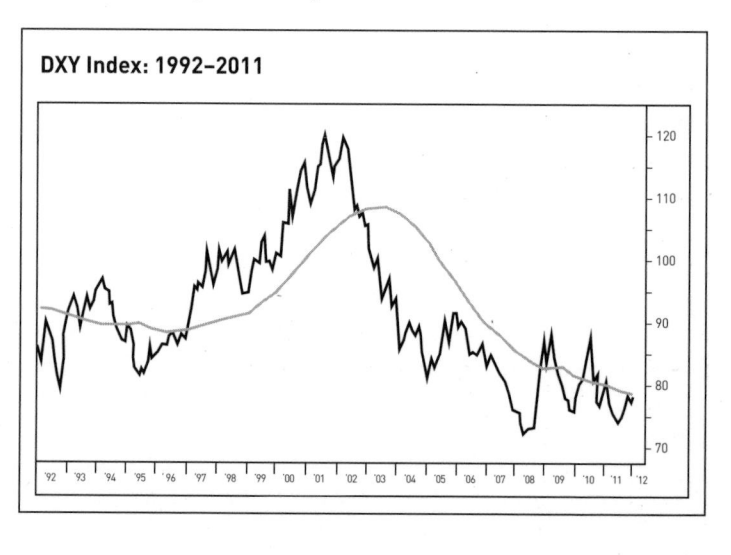

DXY Index: 1992–2011

In recent times, the strategy of the Federal Reserve has been to print an almost unlimited amount of dollars to try and kick-start the economy and create some sort of inflation. The Chairman believes that the lesson of the Great Depression of the 1930s is that without inflation the economy will come to a standstill, which is something that must be avoided at any cost, even if it means undermining the USD.

At the same time, many other countries are worried about the debt burdens they have built up. If they print more money, the value of their debt also falls through the creation of inflation, and their exports become more competitive. As more countries try to lower the value of their currency, it drags in other countries that see their relative competitive situation deteriorating as well, and a vicious circle of currency devaluations can follow.

This is why a lot of people are beginning to worry about the value of all the paper currencies, and this is where gold comes in – there is no way to print the oldest currency in the world. If your view is that you don't like any of the currencies you might decide to just put your money in gold. There is one more problem though – should you buy gold in USD? In euros? In Singapore dollars?

▼ Commodities

Commodities are used in virtually everything around us: from computers to jewellery, from food to transport. Investing and trading in commodities is really a play on two main variables: economic growth and secular growth. If the economy grows there is more demand for raw materials, for example in China, and the more people there are in the world the greater the need to feed, dress, house, transport and entertain them.

The world of commodities is divided into three main areas: energy, metals and agriculture. The table below shows this in more detail.

Energy	Metals	Agriculture
Natural gas	Copper	Cotton
Crude oil	Nickel	Soybeans
Heating oil	Aluminium	Sugar
Gasoline	Gold	Wheat
	Silver	Corn
		Cocoa
		Coffee
		Orange juice
		Live cattle
		Lean hogs

▷ The CRB Index

Even though there are many more commodities the 19 listed above together form an index called the CRB index (officially the ThomsonReuters/Jefferies CRB Index).

The chart below shows how the CRB Index has performed since 2000. Basically it tripled from 2000 until 2008, then lost half its value in about 6 months, and has recovered more than 50% since then. Clearly commodities have performed much better than the stock market over this period and would have made more money for its investors.

And this is exactly why so many people are attracted to trading commodities. But remember there is a huge range of commodities to trade, with some difficult to find (gold), some hard to transport (natural gas), and others hard to grow (cocoa) or perishable (orange juice).

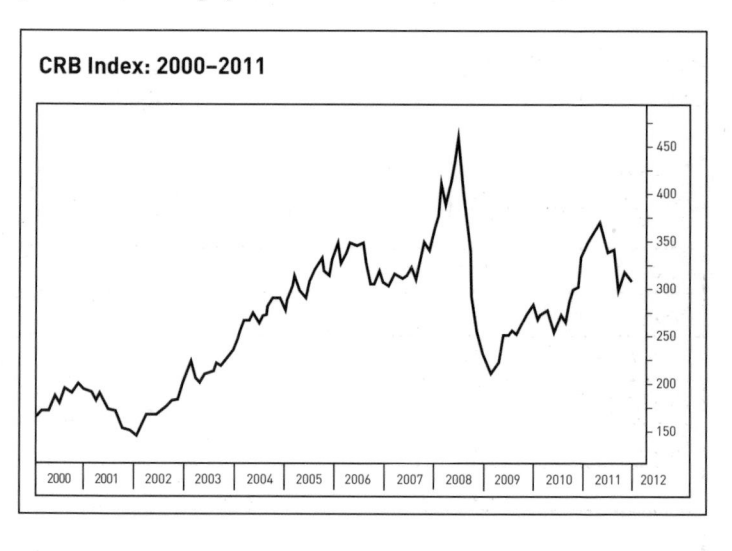

CRB Index: 2000–2011

▷ Trading in commodities

Some people trade commodities because they want to buy or sell the physical goods, while others merely speculate on the direction of the price. The first are known as commercial traders and the latter as non-commercial traders or large speculators. Commercials are producers such as sugar farmers or users of the goods themselves, such as food manufacturers or steel mills. Large speculators tend to be financial companies like commodity funds or hedge funds.

▷ Commodity prices

The price of a commodity is of course decided by demand and supply. And this demand/ supply picture really changes over time. If, for example, there is a big building boom right now, then copper might well be in short supply and copper prices high. If however there are a series of new mining projects coming online a few years down the line, with a corresponding increase in supply, the prices in three years' time could well be a lot lower than the current spot price as you can see on the copper chart below.

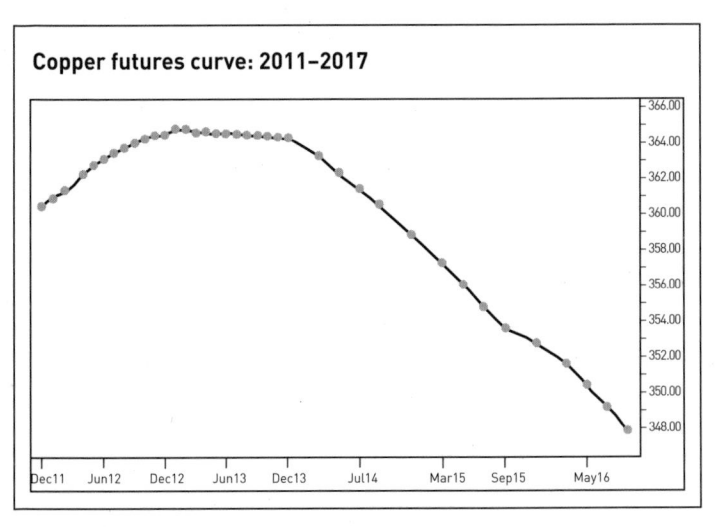

Copper futures curve: 2011–2017

This is why commodities trading tends to be based on futures or forward trading for dates that are sometimes many years into the future. This ensures that producers can hedge their capital intensive projects by selling their products forward and for users to hedge their input costs. And of course it is great for speculators who can bet on long-term price movements without actually having to stock any of the underlying physical goods.

The chart below shows the price of crude oil for delivery for the next seven years. The current spot price is about 102 USD, and the price for the next six months delivery is slightly higher, before sloping down to a crude price of 92 USD in 2016.

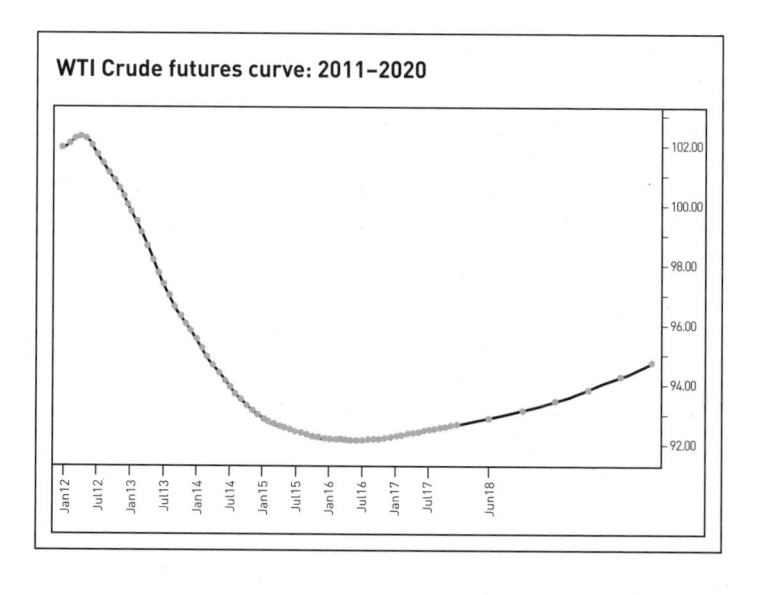

WTI Crude futures curve: 2011–2020

For all commodities you can plot a curve like this, which gives you a good idea of supply and demand in the future. So, if someone tells you that they are bullish on crude oil, a logical question to ask them is for what time frame they are bullish on it.

▷ Market information

Historically market manipulation has had a big impact on the commodities market, as some of the markets can be very illiquid at times, with a small number of parties sometimes controlling large parts of the available supply. There are many stories of market manipulation, the most famous is probably the cornering of the silver market by the Hunt brothers in the 1970s which caused the price of silver to rally from 5 USD in 1978 to almost 50 USD in 1980, before dropping back to 5 USD in 1982! Obviously as an investor you do not want to trade markets that are manipulated by insiders and that is why it is so good that there is data available from the US Commodity Futures Trading Commission (or CFTC), which aims to improve the transparency of the market such as the positions of commercials and non-commercials (but also for the smaller speculators) for many different commodities and often also inventory data of global warehouses.

▷ Net positions

In the chart below there is an example of the net amount (long positions minus short positions) of gold futures held by large speculators, which almost halved between August and October 2011. This information tells you that speculators are much less long than they were before. The gold price actually went down in line with these speculators liquidating their long positions. However, if the gold price had not gone down during this increased selling, this might have been a good sign of inherent strength in the gold price, and you might have concluded that now was a good time for purchasing gold.

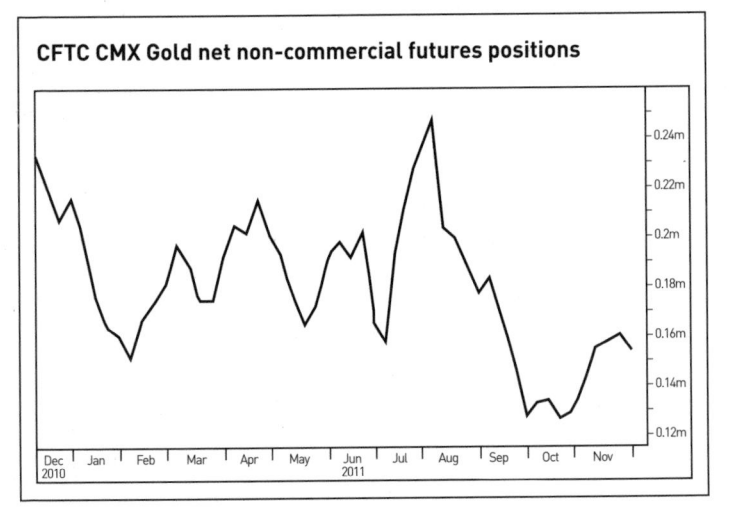

CFTC CMX Gold net non-commercial futures positions

The hope is that this kind of position data can assist in analyzing the underlying commodity. People sometimes say that large positions from speculators are actually less significant than what the commercials are doing because they are the real 'insiders' of a commodity. However, that is not always true because the commercials are the ones who also have to hedge business risk over the whole cycle and might decide to hedge their production even if they are bullish on the underlying commodity. The positions of the small players might be the most significant as they could be seen as a contrary indicator. In any case, these reports are very much analyzed by most players in the market.

▷ Warehouse inventory

Another interesting data series might be warehouse inventory such as the amount of copper stored by the London Metal Exchange. Together with the warehouses in Shanghai they form a large part of the global copper inventories, which are used to back copper futures trading in case a buyer insists on physical delivery of the copper itself. If the amount of stock in the warehouse decreases it could mean that there is real commercial demand for copper and it might pre-empt a price rise. However, the amount of copper that trades for speculative reasons is 50 times larger than the real global demand. This means that even if warehouse inventories go down, the price could still drop if enough speculators keep betting on the price of copper falling, may be because they think that even though current demand might be okay they believe in a slowing world economy going forward.

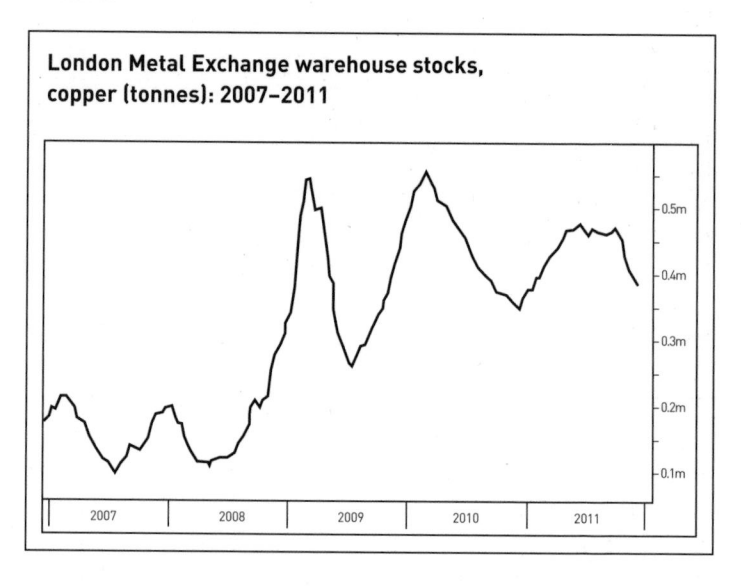

London Metal Exchange warehouse stocks, copper (tonnes): 2007–2011

▷ Commodity analysis

As we discussed earlier, one of the first things to do when analyzing commodities is to look at the forward curve of the commodity itself, which shows the price of the commodity for a number of months in the future.

If the supply and demand situation is relatively stable, generally the price in the future is slightly higher than the current price. This reflects the fact that someone else finances and stores the commodity for you. This can be seen in the chart below, which shows the price of gold for the next five years.

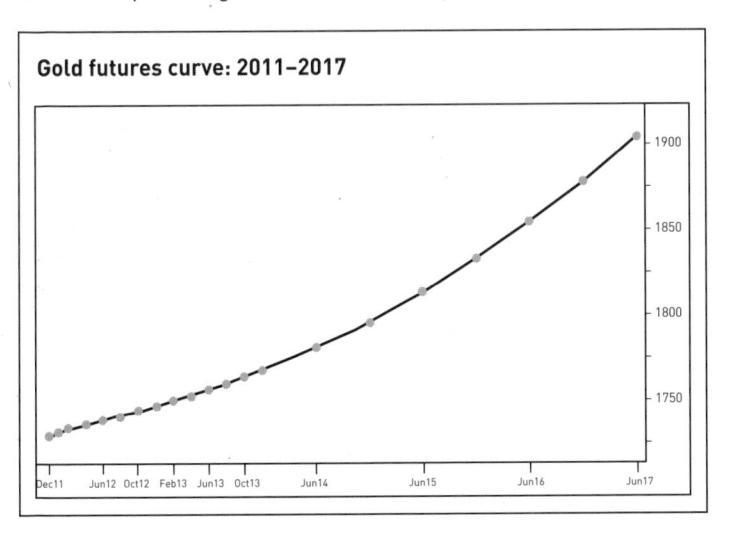

Gold futures curve: 2011–2017

When the 'futures' curve looks like this, it is also known as the commodity being in contango. The opposite situation, as we saw in the previous examples with copper and crude oil, is called backwardation. In addition, some commodities show seasonal patterns as well, such as natural gas, where there is more demand when the weather is really cold, or corn, which has the lowest price just after the harvest and the highest price just before the harvest. Storage costs are a big factor here. The chart right shows the seasonality of natural gas.

As mentioned above, many investors have seen commodity prices go up and have been keen to get exposure to this asset class. However, as I have just demonstrated, it can be quite complicated to do this as one needs to have a good idea of the futures curve before getting involved. If you expect the price of a commodity to go up 10% over the next year but the curve is in contango and already discounts a 10% price rise over the next year, then there

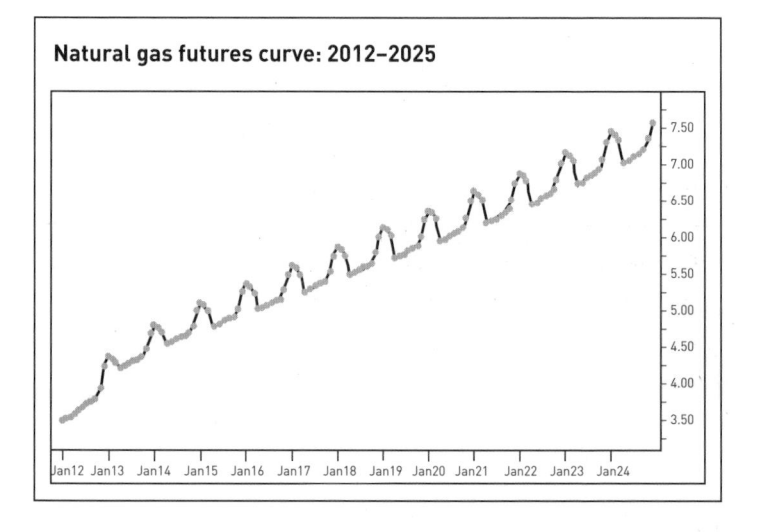

Natural gas futures curve: 2012–2025

really is no trade to be done. However if the curve is in backwardation that might be a great opportunity. Conversely, if you think a commodity will trade down in the future and it is trading in contango that might be a great selling opportunity.

▷ 'Rolling' positions

Futures expire every month or quarter, so it is important to 'roll' your position from one contract that expires, to another contract with plenty of time before expiry. This enables you to avoid delivery of the physical underlying goods (you probably don't want your garden full of sugar), and to avoid strong price movements in the days before a contract expires, as strange price movements often take place in that period based on an oversupply or shortage for delivery.

Clearly most investors don't want the hassle of having to get involved in the futures market and having to move futures contracts forward ('roll') as it is relatively tricky. They might instead buy for example an ETF as a proxy for the underlying commodity as we saw on pp.36–37, or a guaranteed product where a professional manager does the rolling on behalf of the investor (obviously for a fee). Unfortunately this futures rolling is often a real drag on performance (see The Inside Track, below).

For some investors it might just be better to stay away from commodities and do an indirect play by trading fertilizer companies or mining companies instead. For those of you that do decide to trade commodities hopefully you will now be better prepared.

▶ ▶ The inside track
The commodity 'rolling' scam

I have done quite a lot of work on finding a simple way to get exposure to rising commodity prices. I have analyzed structured products from the world's biggest banks and have concluded that you need to be extremely careful before buying commodity products like these.

One of the issues is that the banks tend to roll their futures contracts according to certain schedules that are known to the whole market. For example, they might sell the futures that expire next month to buy the futures that expire the month after that on pre-determined days, say 20% on each of business days 5–9. Other market participants are aware of this, and may well have bought these contracts just slightly earlier and sold them to these banks at an almost riskless profit as they rolled their futures.

It was also apparent that all these banks knew each others' roll schedules and tried to make their own just a little more intelligent, almost like front-running each other. The bottom line though was that the return of many of these products underperformed the actual commodity by such a degree that these products, in my personal view, became uninvestable. And I don't even want to talk about the ETF story on p.37!

▼ What next?

Here we have explored just a few themes relating to currency trading, and some pointers on commodity trading. It is up to you whether you decide to trade in these areas. Something to consider is that whatever country you are based in, holding all your assets in one currency means you are implicitly taking a lot of currency risk anyway, so I would suggest that every person holds at least some foreign currency exposure.

▼ Building a portfolio

Having a balanced portfolio with lots of different ideas and stocks can build you a nice retirement fund. Don't put too much in a single stock or sector, and don't use leverage. Have a cut and respect it.

There is always a story somewhere and usually a way to trade your view. Keep it as pure as possible though and always look at the bigger picture. A company might have a pension deficit, but if there is take-over speculation, the chances are that the stock will rally. A stock might benefit from Sterling falling, but if the underlying business is falling off a cliff as well, the stock will go down no matter what. It is not easy, and rarely black or white – it is all about the odds. Remember, the market will always be around, make sure you are too.

I hope that by now you have a good understanding of how to find investment ideas, how to analyse them and how to build a portfolio. You should also have some idea about the psychological struggles that go on inside the heads of every trader each time they invest. I wish you all the best and most of all: be lucky!

ONCE WE REALIZE THAT IMPERFECT UNDERSTANDING IS THE HUMAN CONDITION THERE IS NO SHAME IN BEING WRONG. ONLY IN FAILING TO CORRECT OUR MISTAKES.

GEORGE SOROS

> Chapter 3

'Million Dollar Traders': putting theory into practice

What could be more fun than putting your money where your mouth is, on television in front of the whole country, with no editorial control?

In early 2009 my television series *Million Dollar Traders*, which was developed with Century Productions, was shown on BBC2. The programme followed a group of eight laypeople, from a variety of backgrounds, as they were given two weeks of training, and then spent the next eight weeks trading on the UK, European and US stock markets. They did not trade fantasy money, it was real money: £500,000 or $1 million (at the exchange rate at that time) of real money. My money.

The training covered the same subjects that have been discussed in this book, and your knowledge at this stage is not dissimilar to what theirs would have been at the end of their training period. The goal was to show that you can pick someone at random, teach him/her the basic rules of trading, and that he/she will perform as well as the experts. It was also meant to show that trading is not just about putting on clever trades but also about the ability to maintain mental composure no matter what.

▶ Million Dollar Traders: a risky trade

This project had a significant personal downside for me. I really was putting my money where my mouth was – not only could the candidates potentially lose a lot of my own money, I also had my professional credibility at stake. Nobody had ever done this before on television.

To make this experiment credible I wanted the candidates to make their own decisions based on what they had been taught. The main instruction was that people made their own decisions and were not influenced by anyone else. They could ask for help whenever they had a purely technical question but not for idea generation and other analysis. I wanted to keep everything as pure as possible.

Obviously I needed the candidates to trade; you cannot make any returns without taking risk and the production company thought it better if the viewers did not fall asleep while watching. The individual candidates had a 20% per stock limit, which is too high for a home-trading situation, but I had a 'portfolio' of eight traders and 20% for them translated into a 2.5% per stock limit for me, which seemed sensible. I was also aware that some of the participants might bring to the table bad habits they had picked up from friends, the media, or so-called 'experts'. One of the candidates had paid to go on an expensive course run by one of these 'experts' and had traded in a small way for his own account for a year. He gave up on that because he lost too much money following the expert's rules. He asked me for some new rules – I told him I wished it were that simple!

You must realise by now that I don't believe in giving people a fixed set of trading rules; not only is it inevitable that the trading environment will change, but I also do not believe that one rule fits each and every trader, as different people obviously have different personalities.

I did not want people in the group to copy one another. Not only because they would learn less, but also because I did not want there to be too much of a consensus in the room. For example, the credit crunch appeared to be a big theme in the portfolios of most of the candidates. This was not exactly original, as it was front-page news in the papers every single day. I was very happy to have a few bets on this theme, but I didn't like the way it seemed to influence every idea. However, I didn't interfere as long as the traders stayed within the risk parameters.

> **THE LOWEST RISK MONEY IS MADE BY LOOKING AT THINGS THAT OTHER PEOPLE HAVE NOT YET LOOKED AT.**

▶ Candidate selection

In the same way that I prefer to run a balanced portfolio of stocks, I also wanted to find a balanced portfolio of traders, each with a different way of looking at situations and finding ideas.

These days it is very hard to get a job as a trader in a bank unless you have an MBA, or a very good university degree. What I have always found fascinating about trading is the fact that a man who sells apples from a market stall might be a better trader than a Harvard MBA or a Cambridge graduate with a double first. That is why when I was trying to put the team together I was really focused on making the group as diverse as possible. I wanted a mix in age, ethnic background and gender. I also preferred people who had never traded before so there would be no time wasted ridding them of bad habits.

I decided to ask everyone exactly the same questions so I could compare like with like. There was also a psychological and numerical test to give me additional information.

I focused my interviews on ten different areas. Each candidate was asked the same specific questions in categories that are based on Lou Adler's book *Hire with your Head* (1998). Some of the questions had a right or a wrong answer; others were just there to help me get a better understanding of the person sitting opposite me. Everybody was filmed while answering these questions, which gave the situation added pressure. Not everybody dealt with this very well which gave me an additional insight into how they might deal with losing real money.

A. Energy, drive, initiative
Is the person able to deal with ten weeks in a highly competitive environment?
1. Why are you here?
2. How did you prepare for this interview?
3. What was on the front page of the *Financial Times* today?

4. What does a trader do?
5. Have you ever traded anything?

B. Trend of personal growth and performance over time
I want candidates who are growing, not people who are too set in their ways to be able to learn new tricks.
6. Tell me about your job.
7. Does the thought of ten weeks of intensive learning, pressure and sleep deprivation scare you?
8. What could make you fail here?

C. Comparability of past accomplishments
I want candidates who have shown the ability to learn and perform a complex task in a short time period.
9. What was the biggest success you had over the last 12 months?
10. What is the most pressure you have ever been under?

D. Education
The candidates must have a certain intellectual capacity to be able to handle a two-week desk based training programme with lots of information to take in.
11. Tell me about your education.
12. What was the last skill that you learned?

E. Problem solving and thinking skills
I need candidates who are able to find solutions to problems and are able to think on their feet.
13. Is your intelligence above average? What percentage of people have above average intelligence?
14. Does the quality of your decision making improve under pressure?
15. How many buses are there in London?
16. What is 32 times 32? (Note confidence on answer.)
17. How many degrees between the hands on the clock at 3.15?
18. If the oil price rises what happens to equity prices?

F. Overall talent, technical competency and potential
I want candidates with the potential to become professional traders.

19. Why would you make a good trader?
20. What is the most money you have ever lost?

G. Management and organisational ability
I like the candidates to be able to handle a task in a systematic, methodical manner.
21. If I gave you £100,000 what would you do with it?
22. What is the most difficult decision you have ever had to make?

H. Team leadership – ability to persuade/motivate others
I need candidates who are able to work in a team.
23. Do you react better to compliments or criticism?
24. How do you deal with authority when you perceive them to be wrong?

I. Character – values, commitment, goals
Honesty, integrity, ethics are key.
25. What would you wear to the office?
26. How are you with money? Are you a big spender? Are you in debt?
27. Would you screw someone over to get ahead?

J. Personality and cultural fit
Is this a person I would like to work with and sit next to 24/7? Is this a person who is able to change his or her mind, or is he or she stuck to a single view?
28. How do you measure success in your life?
29. Why should we hire you and not someone else?
30. If things go wrong do you tend to blame other people or take responsibility yourself?
31. How do you think the interview went? If you were me would you hire you?

Question 16, 'What is 32 times 32', was shown on television. From what I understand a lot of people were worried about that question. All I can say is that to be a good trader it is not necessary for you to calculate it within three seconds; and if you can't calculate it without a calculator it still might not be a problem. It was all about how the manner in which the interviewees answered the 31 questions combined.

▶ The training programme

The training was managed by Raoul Pal, a leading expert on economics and investment strategy, and several parts of this book reflect what he taught the candidates. I was also able to draw upon the expertise of some very experienced City professionals for the training programme.

The two-week training period was intensive to ensure that the traders would learn discipline and follow a portfolio approach to investing. The basic idea was to make sure that nobody would put all their eggs in one basket and that people would try to run their winners and cut their losers. The training the candidates received forms the basis of the eight-step approach for this book. What was very interesting to see was that the candidates made an enormous amount of progress over a very short time period. To quote one of the candidates:

'The initial learning curve was as steep as anything I have experienced – the sheer volume of information I needed to take on board and process was overwhelming, I questioned whether I had the ability to assimilate all this learning but now I feel much better informed and able to base investment decisions on my own opinions of information releases whether they pertain directly to the company (earnings releases) or whether it is knowledge acquired through research or just listening and observing.'

All of the candidates were asked to read a book that I would really recommend, *Market Wizards* by Jack D. Schwager, which contains a series of interviews with profitable traders and analyses what makes them successful. They also kept a diary and wrote a final conclusion. Here are some of their thoughts (on an anonymous basis) to show what they learned, and the type of experience they had.

Each heading relates to the points that form the basis of the investment framework outlined in this book.

1. Understanding the world and the investment environment

'There's an astonishing variety of instruments available across the world for people to trade on a 24-hour basis, and it's no wonder that people can make or lose fortunes in the twinkling of an eye. However, it's almost impossible to make money consistently if you can only trade long or buy real stocks, and it's very difficult to make money even if you can trade short or long as you wish. This is a sobering thought in relation to my private investments and pension fund – a fair proportion of them should probably be in more unconventional instruments such as FX [foreign exchange], commodities and property.'

'In my mind however, the most dangerous characteristic of the system embodied by the "city" and the characteristic that will inevitably lead to its fall or radical evolution is the almost religious and pathological belief in "growth".'

'About the markets? Well number one ... it's horribly fickle and it will kill you if it has the chance.'

2. What we can learn from the past

'I was able to gain a degree of perspective which didn't stop me waking in the middle of the night after a bad day but did ensure I learnt from my mistakes and therefore tried really hard not to repeat them or seek out what relevant points had I missed to get a trade wrong.'

'The data we needed to research for the morning meeting has made me view the world in an entirely different way and I now feel I think more "outside of the box" when I read a news story giving consideration to wider implications than just the content of the story.'

3. Idea generation
'I have learnt that there is always opportunity if you can see it, and that if you are pretty sure then you should probably stand by your convictions.'

'I also find I process information I hear whether in passing or in conversation in terms of what it might mean to a company's share price which will probably make me an incredible bore if I verbalise it to anyone who hasn't gone through this experience. It almost forces you to think about everything in terms of shorts or longs and thus money to be made'.

'I've learnt that you should ALWAYS have a plan and you should NOT deviate ... I have learnt that your views should be consistent and cohesive.'

4. Analysing companies
'Likewise, listening to the tales of experienced fundamental traders was a little like listening to the anecdotes and stories of a master fisherman. Someone whose "feel" for a system can only ever be developed intuitively and through much devotion to its intricacies and tireless ebbs and flows.'

5. Analysing stock movements
'I really enjoyed learning about the "dark arts" of technical analysis though found it ironic that despite the most rigorous reliance on patterns and "flags", we were constantly reminded that this was an art and not a science.'

6. Reality check
'Coming from a position of being a total amateur – reading the money/business pages of *The Sunday Times* and thinking the tips were well placed (ha, ha), not anymore. I fully appreciate how out of date the share tips are in all these papers and web sites and that following their advice is unlikely to make much of a return unless the value of the share has a long way to go (in either direction). In fact, in many cases by the time the news reaches you from these sources of information, the likelihood of doing the

opposite to their recommendations is probably more likely to provide a better return.'

7. Head check
'"Know thyself" remains one of the most important slogans in this business.'

'I have learnt that I am an emotional guy but that's okay ... I am allowed to be emotional and it helps me in many ways, but if I can't control this it has the potential to destroy me.'

'More than that I have learned more about myself. Confirmed that I hate losing, that I can control my emotions even tho' I am kicking and screaming inside.'

'Only by taking a walk round the block did I manage to resist closing the trades and crystallising my losses.'

'Still have to kick myself not to be lazy, and I know that I trade best when I have done the in-depth work on a stock rather than swinging the bat.'

8. Building your portfolio and controlling its risks
'I've learnt that every stock and every company has a story that can be exploited by the right person, but it takes some thinking outside of your ordinary realms to understand how to play the game.'

'I have learnt about risk and how to manage it. I have learnt about looking at the woods and not the trees and that you shouldn't worry too much about single stock movement if you still believe in the trade.'

'... nothing gives you perspective like losing money.'

'The largest factor negatively affecting my quantified performance was my tendency to hold on to losing trades far too long.'

▶ Some observations and some conclusions

Some people performed better than others. One person, even though he was highly intelligent, was keen to put on trades quickly but was not confident in his opinions, and therefore kept getting rid of losing trades before they had the chance to turn around and make money. Cutting substantial losers is one thing, but cutting every time a position shows a loss is quite another. Where this candidate did differ from a typical novice was that he adhered to a certain amount of risk control. He did not put all his eggs in one basket and he did not let his losses accumulate.

Another person – again very intelligent – also lacked confidence. But in this instance it meant the candidate was too scared to put on trades in the first place. I must qualify this by saying that an eight-week period is a very short time over which to draw any significant conclusions but that is all I had to go on.

But some others excelled. They were able to take experience from their own lives, and convert that into original ideas and trades that they felt comfortable with, as they already understood some of the industry dynamics, whether it was leisure goods, beverages or defence companies. They were able to stay composed when things went wrong, even though on the inside they must have been in turmoil. They could do this because they respected and understood risk.

I think the programme was quite successful. Even though it was filmed in one of the hardest markets of recent memory eight inexperienced traders collectively outperformed the professionals; they lost about 2% and the professionals about 4%. I think that at least half the candidates would now be able to manage their portfolio in a safe manner with results that would keep outperforming the experts.

One of the big drags on performance one experiences when giving money to the experts is the number of fees charged for different services. Doing it yourself will give you a head start. The programme demonstrated some of the things you need to be successful: you need to have confidence and know when to cut and when not to cut, and you need to persevere to the end. And don't hang on to bad habits. If you ignore what you are being taught it tends to be a bad trade.

►Be responsible for your own finances

One of the main reasons for writing this book and making the television series is that, in general, people do not take enough responsibility for their finances, often because it seems too difficult or confusing. They would rather leave it to the so-called professionals who tell you they can do it better.

The unfortunate truth is that the professionals have performed very badly for their investors while continuing to charge high fees. The size of the pension fund of the average person in the UK is around £25,000. This is not going to provide many benefits for old age.

The key lesson is that most people can master how to invest responsibly by themselves. It is not about getting rich quickly; it is about getting richer over time. I don't need to make 20% a year, I would just like to make a little bit over many years and never risk losing too much. The mathematics of compounding mean even when you make only 5% or 6% per year you will do really well over

IN THE PROGRAMME WE PROVED THAT WITH THE RIGHT TRAINING YOU CAN OUT-PERFORM THE PROFESSIONALS.

time. You need to learn to control the risks that you take and control the amount of money you are prepared to lose before you want to stop yourself out.

Hopefully this book has given you some of the necessary tools to start investing yourself. Remember, trading or investing is primarily about the protection of your capital, and only secondly about making profits. If only the people that you trusted with your money had the same objectives!

Glossary

Active management: a strategy where a manager makes specific investments with the goal of achieving better returns than a benchmark index such as the FTSE 100. You must believe that the manager and his team are highly skilled before you give your money to an active manager. See also passive management.

Alpha: profit made on a stock because you picked the right stock and the right sector.

Annual general meeting (AGM): a meeting held every year to inform shareholders of what is going on in a company. The company's accounts are presented and resolutions are passed; all shareholders, no matter how small, are permitted to ask questions.

Arbitrage: taking advantage of a price differential between two or more similar stocks.

Asset: everything that is owned by a company, including cash, stock, property and goodwill (an intangible asset).

Bear market: there are different ways to describe a bear market. One commonly used definition is that when a market is trading 20% below its previous highest level, it has entered a bear market. It also tends to be a period characterised by rising unemployment and widespread pessimism.

Beta: profit made on a stock because you picked the right market direction.

Bond: issued by a government or a company to raise money. Interest ('coupon') is repaid every year (or quarter) until maturity, when the principal is repaid. If you own a bond you are lending money to the company, you are not an owner (shareholder) as you would be if you had bought the equity. This means you take less risk but you don't have the same upside as if you owned the equity.

Bottom-up investing: looking at individual companies and making investment decisions based on a company's merits.

Break out: the overcoming of technical resistance. The buyers are more powerful than the sellers who have now run out of ammunition. See also technical resistance.

Broker: a party who acts as an agent in the buying or selling of a stock. These agents need to be registered with the appropriate government bodies.

There are three levels of service:
1. Execution-only service: client makes all decisions, broker just executes.
2. Advisory service: client decides, broker gives advice on specific shares.
3. Discretionary service: broker makes decisions on behalf of the client.

Bull market: a market where prices tend to rise and investors feel good about investing in stocks.

Business cycle: the tendency of economies to move through periods of boom and bust, with fluctuations in economic growth occurring every five years or so.

Commodity: products such as rice, wheat, pork bellies, corn, gold, silver and copper, usually produced by agriculture or mining, that are traded by producers, consumers and speculators.

Compounding returns: it is amazing how much you can make if your return is 6% a year. If you start with £10,000 this will be £18,000 after 10 years and £43,000 after 25 years. At 7% this will be £19,700 and £54,000 respectively. So you do not need to take a lot of risk to do well over time.

Continuation pattern: where a chart continues behaving as before, i.e. it remains within the previous range or trend.

Correlation: a measure of the similarity between two or more stocks.

Currency: legal tender under the jurisdiction of the government that issues it. Some currencies are more important than others, for example, the US Dollar is the most widely accepted currency in the world.

Cut: unwinding your stock position at a loss.

Cyclicals: basic resources, such as oil and copper, which perform well in the markets during upturns as the economy expands, but do badly in downturns as manufacturing capacity stands idle or contracts. That is why these sectors are often called 'cyclicals': they move with the business cycle.

Debt ratio: total assets divided by total liabilities.

Depression: an economic downturn more severe and prolonged than a recession.

Derivatives: financial instruments whose value is based on an underlying asset such as a stock price, an index etc. Two important types of derivatives are futures and options.

Dividend: a payment from a company to its investors, generally out of the profits the company has made over the previous period.

EBITDA: the earnings of a company before interest, taxes, depreciation and amortisation are deducted.

Equity: same as a stock or a share. See also stock.

EV: the enterprise value of the company, which is the debt outstanding plus the equity.

Exchange-traded fund (ETF): an easy and quick way to buy a basket of stocks by purchasing just one stock exchange listed security. Most ETFs track an index, such as the Dow Jones Industrial Average or the FTSE 100, but they can also be an easy way to buy or sell gold or crude oil, or soft commodities such as wheat.

Financial market: a place where people can deal in financial instruments such as stocks, bonds and commodities. Financial markets are continuously evolving and adapting to new technologies and regulations.

Financial Services Authority (FSA): regulates the financial services industry in the UK.

Fundamental analysis: looking at a company from the perspective of its core business model and its finances.

Futures contract: a standardised agreement traded on a futures exchange, to buy or sell a specific amount of a commodity or a security, at a specific price and for a specific settlement date.

Gross Domestic Product: the monetary value of all goods and services produced by an economy over a specified period.

Hedge: a position established to protect the value of another position and reduce risk. If you own (are long) a stock but are worried about the market going down you might want to sell (short) an ETF that tracks the market.

Hedge fund: an investment fund that not only buys securities but also sells short securities. The manager typically charges a management fee and a performance fee. Hedge funds can invest in many different securities such as shares, debt, commodities, wine, property and private businesses.

Index: a single number that represents the performance of a number of underlying securities. The FTSE 100 shows the performance of the largest 100 UK listed companies. In France they use the CAC 40, in Germany the DAX 30, Japan has the Nikkei 225, and in the US the best-known indexes are the Dow Jones, the S&P 500 and the technology based Nasdaq 100.

Investment: not spending your money now, but using it in the form of debt where you are paid interest, or as a share of a company to obtain profits in the form of dividends.

Investment bank: a financial institution that helps companies and governments raise capital, provides advice on mergers and acquisitions, and trades securities for clients or on its own account.

Investment time horizon: the length of time over which an investment is made or held before it is liquidated.

Leverage: investing with borrowed money with the aim of achieving a larger return than you would if you only used your own money.

Liability: everything that is owed by a company.

Margin of safety: the difference between the intrinsic value of a stock and its market price or the price at which a share investment can be bought with minimal downside risk.

Market capitalisation: the total market value of a public company. It equals the stock price multiplied by the number of shares outstanding. FTSE 100 stocks are qualified as large cap(italisation) stocks as opposed to mid-cap and small cap stocks.

Moving average: the average price of a stock or index over the last number of days. If the last five prices were 8, 10, 12, 15, 15, the five day moving average will be 12 and the three day moving average will be 14.

Options: the right to buy or sell a given security at a future date at a certain price. Options can be used for hedging or as a direct investment.

Overbought: when a stock price has risen too much, too fast.

Oversold: when a stock has fallen too much, too fast.

Pair trade: buying one stock and selling another stock, betting on the outperformance of the former.

Passive management: a financial strategy in which one tries to mimic a given index. No real investment decisions are made. The big advantage is that this minimises transaction costs. See also active management.

Portfolio: a basket of investments. The more diversified the basket the lower the risk.

Portfolio management: decisions regarding the composition of a portfolio. This is a function of the risk of the underlying stocks, the way they correlate to one another, timing and total expected return.

Price to book ratio: stock price divided by book value per share.

Price to earnings ratio (P/E): stock price divided by earnings per share. The higher the P/E the more expensive a company.

Profit margin: net income divided by sales.

Recession: a recession exists when an economy has recorded negative growth for at least six months.

Reversal pattern: where a chart changes character.

Secular trends: extremely long term stock market trends either upwards or downwards.

Short selling: selling a stock that the seller does not own at the time of the sale (i.e. the stock is borrowed). The goal is later to buy that stock back at a lower price, thus making a profit on the trade, before giving the stock back to the party it was borrowed from. Short selling can be for outright profit motives or to hedge a position and thus reduce risk.

Speculation: attempting to make a profit while accepting the chance of a loss. If the chance of risk is low, people tend to use the term investment. Speculation thus implies that losses are not improbable. See also investment.

Stock: a stake or share in the ownership of a company. See also equity.

Stock exchange: a market place for shares where buyers and sellers come together.

Stock market bubble: a period of stock market euphoria where stocks trade at ever-higher prices, becoming more and more detached from the underlying economic reality. Every stock market bubble ends in tears, and the timing of this is almost impossible to predict.

Stop (stop-loss): a level of the stock price where a stock position is liquidated. The goal is to contain further losses.

Target price: an analyst's estimate of the price of a stock at some point in the future.

Technical analysis: The study of past market data, primarily price and volume, to predict future stock price movements.

Technical resistance: a level where prices find it hard to trade above. This is normally because of the presence of large sellers.

Technical support: a level at which prices find it hard to trade below. This is often because of a large buying interest.

Tick chart: a chart that shows every single trade that takes place in a given time period.

Top-down investing: focusing on building a general opinion of the economy and the world and then building a portfolio of stocks that fit within this picture.

Transaction cost: a commission payable to the broker to pay for their services.

Volatility: the amount that a stock has moved over the past time period. It is often used to predict the risk of the stock over a future time period.

Volume: the amount of shares that trade on any given day.

Index

C

D

E

F

Acknowledgements

I would like to thank the following for all their help and support: Chris Banse, Richard Barnett, Tim Bullman, Harald Cataquet, Katie Chapman, Paul Cooper, Kate Cornet, Katie Cowan, Neil Daldy, Ilya Davar, Robin Dixon, Simon Dunitz, Candy Han, Cedric Hanisch, Katie Hewett, Harry Holzer, Clive Jackson, Bruce Kaminsky, Andreas Klaingutti, Anton Kreil, Dawn and Gary McClure, Robert Miller, James Montier, Jurjen Munting, Maureen Murphy, Anthony Phillipson, Ruth Pitt, Joel Roodyn, Severine Saing, Mushtaq Shah, Marc Slendebroek, Karl Thompson, Khoi Tu, Clare Turner, Jacob and Vivien de Tusch-Lec, Simon and Martha van Dam, Simone van der Kamp, Graham Ward, Talia Watson, Steve Ward, Geoff Wilkinson, Steve Wreford, Marilyn Zwaaf and most of all Mary Turner.

Particular thanks must go to Raoul Pal. Raoul managed the training programme for *Million Dollar Traders*. He has been a friend and colleague of mine for many years and his logical thinking has made a significant contribution to many of the sections of this book. His publication *The Global Macro Investor*, is read by many of the world's biggest hedge funds, banks and investment funds.